Presented to: _____

By: _____

Date _____

The Coffee Lover's Guide

The Coffee Lover's Guide

Great Coffee

The Coffee Lover's Guide

Kevin Sinnott

Bridge-Logos *Publishers*

Gainesville, Florida 32614 USA

Great Coffee

By Kevin Sinnott

Copyright 2001
by Bridge-Logos Publishers
Library of Congress Catalog Number: Pending
International Standard Book Number: 0-88270-841-4

Published by:
by **Bridge-Logos** *Publishers*
Gainesville, FL 32614
http:/www.bridgelogos.com

Printed in the United States of America. All rights reserved.
Under International Copyright Law, no part o fthis publication may be reproduced, stored, or transmitted by any means-electronic, mechanical, photogrphic (photocopy), reocroding, or otherwise-written permission from the Publisher.

"Fill me up, Johnnie."

Consumer coffee expert Kevin Sinnott visits a roaster

Great Coffee author KEVIN SINNOTT may be reached for speaking engagements at 312-656-7620.

Kevin Sinnott has a collection of fifty coffee makers and grinders and often brews coffee thirty times per day. A stickler for detail, he rates coffee makers only after a minimum thirty days active testing. A thumbs up review by Sinnott is a highly sought prize in the industry due to his thoroughness and honesty. He publishes the *Coffee Companion* newsletter. His latest projects include www.coffeecompanion.com on the worldwide web and several national media tours as a spokesperson for great coffee. Sinnott lives in pastoral seclusion in Warrenville, Illinois, with his wife Patricia and their three children.

Coffee Contents

15   25   35   43   61

www.bridgelogos.com

Short Shots		15
Coffee Inspiration/Devotionals:		17-177
1	Why Great Coffee (isn't all coffee great?)	25
2	Finding the Best Bean Varieties for You	35
3	Roasting: What it Means to You	43
4	Fresh Coffee Checklist	53
5	All-time Greatest Coffee Makers	61

Coffee Contents

6	Brewing	73
7	Great Coffee Out	89
8	Coffee Collecting	95
9	Espresso History and Drinks	105
10	Coffee Recipes	115
11	Coffee, Caffeine and Health	131
12	Politics and Bean Counts	141
13	Coffee Myths	147

Rainy Day Features Section

14	Coffee on Television	161
	Coffee in the Movies	165
	Coffee Behind Bars	166
	My Christmas Cup	171
15	Coffee on the Web	175
16	Coffee Questions and Answers	181

Acknowledgments

I would like to thank the following kindred spirits for their help with my coffee studies and research throughout my journey to discover the perfect cup.

The Specialty Coffee Association of America's Executive Director Ted Lingle, who always takes my calls and he likes coffee as strongly brewed as I do. Ted gave us permission to use the Association's classic coffee line drawings, and also provided illustrations from William Ukers' 1935 book, *All About Coffee*.

Ian Bersten - Author of *Coffee Floats, Tea Sinks*, who's been my closest intellectual support. Together we've built a new wing on the phone company due to long distance bills between Chicago and Sydney. Ian supplied the classic percolator photos in Chapter Eight on Coffee Collecting.

Richard Hagan - Richard has graciously shared with us his classic collection of coffee advertising from the Pan-American Coffee Bureau (now defunct) and oldcoffeeroasters.com/robots.htm on the internet. Take a look at Old Coffee Roasters.com on the internet. I agree that "good things happen over coffee."

My brother John. Thanks to he and I owning identical vacuum coffee makers, we're possibly the only two people able to discuss coffee as wine and be reasonably sure of our results.

Ken Stevenson - Ken was the first person who, years ago, I telephoned asking for help writing my first newsletter. It was he who flew me out to Denver the next day and from there to Seattle to show me his industry first-hand. If I've helped the industry, it is Stevenson whom the industry owes thanks.

Jane McCabe - Ms. McCabe, who edits and publishes the *Tea and Coffee Trade Journal*, has always been a good friend and editor. She tolerates my personality.

Shea Sturdivant - Fellow coffee writer and just a wonderful friend. She's one of the few people in my life who I've overheard saying something good about me. She's encouraged me when I really needed it and is a one-woman coffee-promotion board.

Patricia Fitzgibbon Sinnott - She's given up her house to coffee research for nearly ten years, all while raising our family (probably including me). She is my constant reminder that friendship is deeper than any coffee roast.

Ken Davids - Fellow coffee writer. Anytime, any place, anything Davids writes about coffee is okay with me. We've spent a lot of time together and we disagree about almost everything, but we agree the we enjoy each other's writing and we agree about our mutual love of the bean and its wonderful liquid extraction.

Marianne Graves - You know I can't spell, remember anything and I'm always in hurry. Yet you've helped through this whole process, without ever losing your quiet, calm and charming personality.

I've decided I can't thank any one person who roasts, sells or manufactures equipment. They're all too nice, and too competitive. I'd never be able to live with myself if I missed one of my many friends. But, thanks for all of the free samples. I can be bought, but I can't be bored.

Kevin Sinnott
January 2001

Introduction

My devotion...to God...to coffee

Hey, what's "religion" doing in a coffee book? Hmmm. Well, I could say that I'm just trying to give the *New York Times* a reason to review yet another coffee book, but I must say there is a purpose.

When I first began to write the *Coffee Companion* newsletter, I also began to develop my spiritual side. It was as if each development was connected to the other. Finally, it began to dawn on me that they are connected. To be direct, the more I have found the love of Christ in my everyday life, the more I devote to serving others, the greater my sense of enjoyment in all things.

Coffee is very much a drink of history. It is a drink of the present. And, I'm inclined to believe it will be a drink of the future as well.

Like coffee, Christianity has experienced its share of dark ages, where it's wonderful attributes were overshadowed by political and social misunderstanding. I know of no Christian who wants to return to the dark ages, just as I know of no coffee connoisseur who wants to go back to the electric percolator.

A friend of mine put it nicely: "You can only talk relationships and politics over so many cups of coffee. Eventually, you have to move on to bigger topics."

What bigger topic is there than God? And, for 2000 years, for most of the Western World, when you're talking God, you're talking Christ.

Foreword

Why another coffee book?

I'll tell you right off, I'd rather be brewing than writing. I love coffee. Not typing. If you go to a bookstore, you'll see right away the various coffee titles sandwiched between beer and cooking in the Foods category.

Some of these books are fun to read. Several influenced me when I became interested in drinking great coffee. Ken Davids' landmark *Coffee* is a great romantic look at coffee from a lovable hippie/professor/poet. I've met and in fact collaborate with Professor Davids. We share coffee's romance but I feel the picture is incomplete without some further practical tutorials on how to use the gear.

It's a great irony. Ken is the teacher and I dropped out of school and I'm the one pushing for strict disciplines in brewing. But, the truth is coffee doesn't come ready. You have to make it.

And, that's what compels me to finish the story. None of the coffee books I've found really helped me make great coffee. Find it yes. Brew it, no way.

I intend to give you power that I've spent the last ten years refining in my own life. I am able to go into a coffee store, sniff around until I find some fresh beans and then take those beans home, grind them and brew coffee from them that really tastes like it smells. I happen to own a substantial amount of gear, but most of it is unnecessary. I use a grinder, and a simple brewer. I can do it out of town, with a tiny travel kit.

It's not brain surgery, but it takes a little information. As a friend of mine who is a surgeon once told me when "a man who knew how to do surgery showed me how he did it and now I do it."

Same with coffee. **Read on.**

Coffee Gallery

Short Shots

Pan-American Coffee Bureau circa 1953

"Time Out, Johnny - Mom's making Coffee!"

Coffee Inspiration

Coffee Business Adage

"Never pour coffee towards anyone."

LORD, WHY DID YOU PUT THIS BEAN IN MY LIFE?

There I was, sitting with my friend Larry McManus in a Dunkin' Donuts in 1993. I began talking about my view of Dunkin' Donuts versus Starbucks. About two points into my diatribe, I noticed Larry was making out a "to-do" list for me.

"Here," he said, handing the notes he'd scribbled to me. "I've heard enough about coffee. Why don't you write a newsletter about coffee?"

Then he leaned toward me as if to keep secret his final admonishment.

"Tell someone new about it."

That night I went home and, laptop in hand, sat in my kitchen, writing a flurry of opinions I'd picked up since I'd begun personally researching coffee many years before.

Classic coffee cans

Short Shots

What Do Coffee Bubbles Mean?

Bubbles appear to form in the center when weather will be fair. If they form at the sides, it means rain. If they scatter all over, the weather will change. Strangely, meteorologists appear to confirm this. The science is attributed to the way air pressure affects coffee's surface tension. Betcha didn't know that your cup of coffee is also a weather vane.

Be sure to use a cup of strong coffee. Weak or instant coffee doesn't work.

To Pour or Not to Pour...

A study was recently done to study that age-old coffee argument: To keep coffee hot longer, should you pour the cream in first, or is it better to pour the cream just before you drink it? Every commuter wants to know this in order to keep his or her coffee warm. Turns out that study said you should pour the cream in as soon as possible after the coffee is poured from the carafe. That keeps the coffee warmer, longer.

Stretching the Truth

Innovative consumers packaging of the year – rubber bands! Anyone who buys coffee in usually paper sacks knows how hard it is to keep container airtight. Short of innovative packaging ideas (don't hold your breath) the best and easiest way to keep beans fresh in their original container is by putting a rubber band around the length of the package. The constant pressure keeps air squeezed out more effectively than by using the built-in twist tie. My recommendation is the number sixty-four rubber bands. I think I paid sixty-nine cents for a package of sixty. Oh, they're 100% natural, the overused cliche of the century.

New Sugar!

How fond we are of Nutrasweet, the almost no calorie sweetener used in coffee. Now there's a new competitor called Sucralose. Like aspartame (Nutrasweet's generic sweetening component) Sucralose is many times sweeter than sugar. Its makers claim, however, that Sucralose will not buckle during prolonged heating, not a problem in coffee but definitely one in baking and other uses. What remains to be seen is whether Sucralose duplicates Nutrasweet's fruit flavor enhancing qualities. Since coffee is, in fact, derived from a fruit, it has always been my opinion that it outperforms sugar itself in the cup. Some form of sweetener is used in nearly 80% of all coffee beverages consumed, at least according to our random sampling.

Meanwhile, Equal has been putting the "improved taste" label on its package for some time. Is it improved? I think so, though I can't find out why. It appears to be stronger, which makes me wonder if they've simply increased the aspartame to inert substance ratio.

Short Shots

First North American Coffee Bar

Did "Seattlelites" discover espresso? New Yorkers? Guess again. The first North American espresso machine was installed in The Sidewalk Café, Toronto Canada. The year? 1956.

Lloyd's of London a Café?

The famed insurer Lloyd's of London did in fact start out as a coffeehouse. Apparently, the seagoing personnel who would drop in for a cuppa joe were given to gossiping about business. The savvy Lloyd's management began betting on one ship or another making it through, which is what insurance is after all. Just another example of a company having the sense to move where the profit is.

Blessed Cafe

A Mother Teresa look-a-like cinnamon bun recently appeared at the Bonga Java cafe in Nashville, Tennessee. My first thoughts upon hearing this were that this was some kind of publicity stunt, but the photos on the internet were convincing. Besides, when the shop owner told me they offer a bookmark and prayer card for $1.50 my heart was completely won over. It's just like Mother Teresa to appear at an independent cafe and not some major chain.

Coffee Tweak Department

Wanna upgrade your coffee maker for sixty-nine cents? I know it sounds hard to believe but I've done it. What it is, is food-grade ascorbic acid. The principle is that your coffee maker builds up calcium deposits through regular use. Every electric drip coffee maker has a hot water pipe inside. What I notice happening is that a gradual buildup in the pipe quickly affects the PH balance of the hot water, which means it affects the flavor of the brew. All I know for sure is that after cleaning several coffee makers (one that was relatively new) the coffee flavor immediately changed for the better.

Toothpastes to Avoid with Coffee

Commercial toothpastes contain an overpowering and taste-dulling ingredient that lasts for around twenty minutes. This presents a dilemma to those who brush right after breakfast, but before having their morning cup of coffee. Solution: Buy homeopathic toothpaste from your local health food store. Since homeopathic drugs can be rendered useless by anything strong tasting, these toothpastes cannot contain strong spice tastes.

Coffee Shortens Life? Not Here!

Coffee taster Sidney Kinnell, who traveled to Europe to find the right beans to develop a Mocha-Java blend for visiting English King George the VI, died at age 93. He always drank tea with meals and avoided all spices, onions and cigarettes. Once, a friend sent him the same coffee sample two months apart to test his abilities. Kinnell called the amused colleague with, "Ah, thought you had me, eh?"

Lawyers and Coffee

Donald Horowitz, Esq., sued a Newark, New Jersey restaurant in 1994 after he was served a double espresso by mistake! According to Mr. Horowitz, the coffee was supposed to be decaf and it put him into the hospital with a rapid heartbeat.

Short Shots

Famous Coffee Drinkers

Pope Clement - No one now remembers a single thing about him except that he took one sip from his coffee cup and smacked his lips together, creating an ecumenical bond between Christians and the Moslem coffee merchants.

Orson Welles - Welles is remembered as one of the most ornery filmmakers of all time. It is not known whether coffee irritated him or he just didn't have enough good stuff. Welles is remembered as having a personal midget servant travel with him and personally prepare his blend of Mocha-Java.

Serving Coffee at a barber shop in Cairo

Raymond Burr - Burr (as Perry Mason) is said to have rivaled Jack Webb for title of "drinks most coffee on television." The *Perry Mason Show's* constant depictions of Mason drinking late night cups with secretary Della Street and detective sidekick Paul Drake convinced an entire generation to drink coffee morning, noon and night.

Greta Garbo - Miss Garbo, whose seeming inability to speak clear English always seemed to clear up when negotiating her studio contract, was one of the first stars to demand (and get) perks (pun intended) like freshly brewed coffee at all times in her dressing room. She, of course, being Scandinavian predisposed her to prefer a light-roasted blend that clarified coffee's acidity. Her MGM studio vacuum coffee machine was auctioned off long ago for an undisclosed price.

Oprah Winfrey - Like most high-powered entrepreneurs, Ms. Winfrey is predisposed to drinking massive amounts of high-energy coffee. In her case, she has a strong affinity for Starbucks Mocha Cappuccino. Rumor has it that Starbucks considered putting a store just across the street from Winfrey's Harpo productions in Chicago just to satisfy their co-venturist's cravings. Harpo's staff instead got their boss to allow them to get some high end coffee right in the office. This apparently ended when the Harpo folks started noticing more coffee than productivity. (Italians invented espresso to reduce coffee breaks in their new socialist society).

What will Winfrey do next? This is a coffee book, not a tabloid. But, I'll be watching too.

Mel Gibson - Committed Christian, family man and number one heartthrob Mel Gibson loves coffee. Rumorists claim he insisted that lines about his character's coffee romance be added to the film *Conspiracy Theory* in order to make the role easier to play. Knowing his Australian roots would indicate someone who prefers lighter roasted coffee, but strong and fresh. My female friends keep suggesting I invite him over for some brew, just so they can watch him sip coffee and dream (them, not Mel). I will if Mrs. Gibson comes along, too.

Coffee Gallery

Chapter One

Why Great Coffee (Isn't All Coffee Great?)

Pan-American Coffee
Bureau circa 1953

Good Things Happen With Coffee

Courtesy of the Specialty Coffee Assn. of America

The Coffee Tree as pictured by La Roque in his "Voyage de L'Arabie Heureuse"

Coffee Inspiration

"The World of the generous gets larger and larger. The world of the stingy gets smaller and smaller." Proverbs 11:24

So, how does this apply to coffee? Easy. One of the great things about coffee is it's impossible to collect. Unlike wine, artwork and antiques all coffee is limited. It is like beauty. You enjoy the present and look forward to memories. Therefore, coffee is something shared. I find myself giving away cups and even beans all the time. Why not? It won't last. There's no such thing as a vault for coffee. The few times I've accidentally stored some coffee, I felt sad when I found it again. Such a shame. No one finished the bag when it was fresh. Even the best coffee in the world must be consumed. So, generosity and coffee go hand in hand.

1

Why Great Coffee
(Isn't All Coffee Great?)

Some smart aleck always asks, "Isn't all this gourmet coffee stuff smoke and mirrors?"

As a man who genuinely tries to be a good Christian, I am compelled to give you the honest truth: Most of the coffee sold in the U.S. is good coffee. Of course, there's a saying that the enemy of good is great.

As far as the "smoke and mirrors" part goes, yeah, there's some of that. In commodity coffee, it means slapping a label on a sack of beans that says "gourmet" or "estate." Even at the high end, I know a roaster who says one of his competitors simply labels any coffee "Costa Rica." I must say that the majority of people at the "specialty" sector are pretty fastidious... to a fault. By that I mean they sometimes turn into ultra snobs.

I'm more of an end result kind of guy myself. Take Dunkin' Donuts for example. Now, buy a sack of beans from a Dunkin' Donuts. I used to bribe the waitresses to sell me beans before they formalized their business. There are plenty of broken beans, there are all different sizes and shapes. In terms of specialty coffee these guys don't rate at all. They're like a bar band auditioning for the symphony orchestra. Yet I mean to tell you that Dunkin' Donuts are masters of blending beans where the sum total is better than the parts. I'd take Dunkin's blend over many small batch roasters' house blends.

Too often in the high end, a roaster, especially an honest one, is compelled to offer too many coffees and each one is expected to be the pinnacle of the crop. Sometimes the Kenyas just aren't happening. I've had roasters tell me, "I found a Colombian Excelso that tasted better than the Supremo, but my bins all say Supremo." Consumers don't know that Excelso is a size grade, not a real taste grade.

So, now that you're as confused as the industry, what can you do?

Do what I do. I buy on smell. Of course, there are coffees that are more aromatic than others so it's not totally fair, but I've found it still the best system for finding the best beans. There are all kinds of variables that the industry uses to promote coffees but, for the most part, consumers can't use them as true guides to quality.

Coffee Terms

Here are a few coffee terms used over the years to market quality to consumers (followed by my views):

Mountain Grown – Who hasn't heard this one? Folgers has used it forever. Most coffee is mountain grown. While altitude is a factor, some mountains are higher than others. Some of the finest coffee in the world is Yemen Mocha, which is grown at virtual sea level.

100% Arabica – Yes, this is important. Arabica (arab-beak-uh) is definitely superior to Robusta (row-bust-uh). Robusta wasn't even planted on farms until a disease ruined some arabica fields. Robusta will grow anywhere. After World War II the commodity coffee companies switched to robusta for cost cutting. It's considered a bare minimum in the mainstream for a blend to be all-arabica. Now, in espresso, the ground rules change completely (see espresso).

Dark Roast – Not a sign of quality at all but a roaster decision. Starbucks has a display in virtually every one of their stores that implies that dark roasting is a virtue. It is their choice, no problem. But, some of the worst coffee in the world is dark roasted. In fact, I would argue that light roasted coffee, like sushi, highlights flaws more readily, forcing light roasters to choose their coffees more carefully. Dark roast coffees are not significantly lower in caffeine, another claim.

Estate Grown – What does this really mean? I'm not honestly sure. In some cases, it means a small family-owned farm. This may mean more care is taken in cultivation, but it's no guarantee of quality.

Shade Grown – So named because each small coffee tree is shaded by a second larger tree, giving the coffee extra protection from harsh sunlight each day. This growing method costs real estate and extra care and so it is genuine value-added. The only unfair part is that some coffees cannot be labeled shade grown even though they are automatically shade grown, such as some mountain grown coffees, or Hawaiian coffees, where diffuse sunlight is part of the climate.

Organic – There are so many arguments regarding organics that I don't know where to begin. First, almost no one in the coffee industry believes that organic has anything to do with taste. It comes down to political beliefs and social justice issues, and maybe health. Here's what you may not know. A lot of coffee, particularly small family farm coffee, is not labeled organic when it is, simply due to the relatively high cost of third party certification. Friends in the coffee biz who know tell me this is quite common.

Coffee botanicals – Like all good crops, coffee has been cultivated. Coffee bourbon (burr-bone) is the original coffee. It takes up a lot of space to grow and extra care, and yield. There are newer growths called catura (cuh-tur-uh) and typica (typical without the "l") that grow more efficiently. Most of those in the coffee business would say bourbon is packed with a more powerful taste. This information is virtually useless, however, because coffee is almost never labeled with such information for consumers. This is interesting because the difference between a bourbon and a catura is said to be much more pronounced than between an organic and a non-organic. So goes the business.

Some countries such as Costa Rica have almost nothing but the newer types. Yemen, for instance, has mostly bourbon.

Does the region really mean so much?

This is a very good question. Regions do mean something. Even though all the world's coffee is botanically similar, (bourbon, catura and typica are cultivations of the same basic plant), where coffee grows makes a big difference. Soil, sunlight, temperature...it all makes a difference. So does how the coffee is processed. There is wet and dry processing, and different versions of both methods. Often this varies by region, depending upon the country's commitment to modernizing or for social reasons. Some growing regions use sophisticated methods of processing the coffee, others still have coffee dried on hut roofs. Every aspect makes a taste difference, but few of these variables are known to consumers, sometimes not even to the roaster. They may be interesting, but they don't help to choose coffee.

It is a fact that Sumatran coffees tend toward a certain flavor footprint. To say that all Sumatran coffees taste identical is not true, however.

Roast

Roast – as important as where the coffees come from and how they're grown. Roast is so important that I've given it its own chapter. Suffice it to say here that such terms as air roasted, flame roasted or small batch roasted do mean something, although they are not automatically conclusive evidence that you'll like the coffee.

Aged – Aged coffees are a rarity in today's quick buck world. My wife works for a company whose idea of a senior team leader is someone who's been there six months. It's the same thing in today's coffee market. I've alluded to a spectacular aged coffee I had once from Jim Reynolds at Peet's. Aged means a green, unroasted coffee stored in climate-controlled conditions. Aged coffees were discovered in the olden days, when ships that sailed the long way home from Java to Holland got a reputation for delivering better coffee.

Packaging – Nowhere is there more room for improvement in coffee taste than packaging. It's a dry, unromantic subject but coffee is simply not a product that stores well by nature. Inside the industry, it's pretty much accepted that ten days (!) from roasting is the ideal window of opportunity for the best flavor. That's not very long, is it?

There are methods of storage, some better than others. From a commercial point of view, the practical methods involve finding ways to keep coffee oxygen-free for as long as possible. This means no cans. Canned coffee cannot be packed until the coffee is stale. The process for preparing coffee for canning is even called staling. If coffee doesn't release a lot of its aroma before canning, the can will deform.

Even bean coffee is subject to going stale. The best methods right now involve shooting nitrogen into locking bags while just-roasted coffee beans are tossed inside. The nitrogen chases away the oxygen. Once the bag is sealed, a one-way valve allows the nitrogen and the coffee's naturally releasing carbon dioxide to escape without oxygen getting back in. To say it halts staling is untrue, but it slows it down.

Probably the company that has done the best job of packaging is Illy, the espresso company. Their coffee is so well packaged that some actually believe it gets better in storage, probably the first time in history anyone has said that about roasted coffee.

Now you know more, possibly more than you wanted to know, about coffee terms as they might be used to sell you coffee.

Coffee Gallery

Chapter Two

Finding the Best Bean Varieties for You

Meet the person who works to bring you your morning wake-up. Hint: the beans probably will become a perfect cup of coffee

Photo courtesy of Jaime Fortuno, Yaucco Selecto Coffee Puerto Rico

Courtesy of Specialty Coffee Assn. of America

The Coffee Tree showing details of flowers and fruit

Coffee Inspiration

Great gifts mean great responsibilities. The greater the gift, the greater the responsibilities." Luke 12:48

Luke isn't known as a coffee connoisseur, but he well might have been. When I find a superb, or great, coffee, I feel compelled to take great care to store it, measure, grind and brew it properly. I recently obtained a truly wonderful Ethiopian Harar. It had that true "winey" touch that distinguishes great coffees from that region. I found myself using my most precious vacuum method to brew it. The flavor was just right and I didn't want to risk a single bean brewing it in a casual manner.

2

Finding the Best Bean Varieties for You

A Few Of My Favorites Single Origin and Blends

So far, I've avoided getting personal about different coffee beans. I'm trying to avoid the tired cliches so rampant in coffee brochures. The truth is, there are fine examples of coffee from just about everywhere the coffee grows on our planet. I've had some lousy coffee from most of these same places.

There are a few generalizations that should help you to find your way around the coffee store.

Colombia – Colombia's coffee is highly promoted, so highly that it's easy to believe that the hype is all they've got. The conventional wisdom that "the better the advertising, the worse the product" doesn't apply here. Some Colombian coffees are as good as the game. Colombia is really an example of a country that took coffee seriously early in the game and has kept at it. About my only knock is that they used to more or less force the growers to put their crops together. The fact it tasted as good as it did is a testimonial to their overall high quality level. That's changing however. I've had some Colombian coffee that's just fantastic. I usually like it lighter roasted, by the way. Don't automatically choose supremo over plainer-sounding excelso Colombian coffee. The "supremo" designation is a size grade, not related to taste.

Ethiopia – Ethiopia is the birthplace of coffee, at least we think it is. Ethiopian coffee can't help but taste different. There are old cultivation and processing methods that refuse to go away, possibly because Ethiopia is poor enough to lack the kind of investment in new technologies. Meanwhile, the climate itself is unique... it's too dry. All this leads to a pretty unique quality in Ethiopian coffee. There are three types of Ethiopian coffee, each distinctive. Yergachefe, Harar and Sidamo. Each is interesting and worth a try. I know people who drink Ethiopian coffee exclusively.

Yemen – Right down the interstate from Ethiopia is Yemen. Yemen coffee is even more intense than Ethiopia. I once witnessed a brawl between two coffee experts about whether Yemen coffee qualified as one of the greats because there are so many things wrong with it. One thing that's right is it's all from old stock growths. The beans are tiny, but tend to be packed with flavor. The beans are irregular, which frustrates roasters, but their extra work will pay off for you in the cup. Yemen is one of the few coffees I can stand to taste dark roasted. It's definitely a love/hate coffee. I love it.

Sumatra – I was once asked in a radio interview to name my dessert island favorite coffee. I didn't miss a beat. Sumatra coffee is a sleeper coffee. It is exceptionally rich and is known for the heaviest body in the biz. Body is the perception of viscosity, like a broth compared to water. Sulawesi coffees are close to Sumatras in overall taste profile. Some say they are superior, but that may be because they are more easily available than the better-known Sumatrans.

Mexico – To borrow a finance term, Mexican coffee is undervalued. Maybe it's because Mexico is so close to the U.S. that there's less romance. Too bad. Some Mexican coffee is very, very good.

Hawaiian – Hawaii produces the famed "Kona" coffee. Kona is noteworthy as the most counterfeited coffee of all time. In 1995 a scandal resulted where tons of Costa Rican coffee had been regularly and for years brought into Hawaii, relabeled and sold as 100% Kona. I remember a roaster friend telling me that he probably learned to cup Kona coffee using Costa Ricans. A man went to prison and a highly-placed female coffee executive went back to her maiden name in order to stay in the coffee business. Consumer lesson #1: Don't pay outrageous prices for coffee. Consumer lesson #2: Costa Rican coffees are a real bargain.

Costa Rica – Costa Rica coffee is some of the most cultivated coffees. Costa Rica uses predominantly new growths, but they've done such a swell job doing it, they are true coffee overachievers. La Minita is noteworthy as one of the few "brands" in the green coffee world, a combination of some great coffee and great marketing. There are other equally fine coffees. I sometimes find that Costa Rican coffees, while otherwise excellent tasting, are a little weak. This is solved by using more grounds per cup.

Guatemala – Guatemala coffees are known for a certain smokiness. This quality is believed to be a result of the mechanical dryers used in processing. Meanwhile, Guatemala produces some fine coffees, some experts say the finest of all the Central Americans.

Jamaica Blue Mountain – A famous coffee, more for its highly commanded price. Yes, there's some good, rich volcanic soil. Unfortunately, the best of the crop goes back to Japan. Once in a while, I've had some truly great Blue Mountain, but most of it has been good, not great. Atlanta coffee great, John Martinez, is one guy who gets it right, mostly because he's descended from Jamaican plantation owners and seems to know how to get the good stuff. Otherwise, buyer beware!

Java – The best Javas are, for the most part, Sumatrans. They probably always were. The Java coffee trade simplified the whole business by simply lumping in good Sumatrans into their shipments. I have an 1871 coffee textbook that says, "the best Javas are from the Mandeling district". That's like someone in Europe reading, "the best New York comedians are in Chicago" (actually a true statement). Java is a great name, in fact it's the slang name for all coffee. Java coffees were reputedly special at one time. The Dutch had beefed up the farming both there and in Pennsylvania (slightly different time periods). Just to seal the deal, the Dutch developed the world's first marketed blend, Mocha-Java, which allowed a roaster to cut the cost considerably by using one third expensive Yemen Mochas and two third's Java. It's a combination that remains and is probably the best way to utilize Javas today. What happened? Two things. First, a rust leaf disease came through Java and killed a lot of the crops, only to be replanted with cheap, and inferior but hardier, robustas. Second, World War II saw the fields being bombed. Since I'm American, I'll say the Japanese did it.

Papua New Guinea – A relatively new coffee in the trade, Papua New Guinea has a lot going for it, mostly as a total rather than any truly distinctive trait. It's like a great ensemble actor… fits into every part but not a leading man. I've had some very good coffee, and it's a young crop. Maybe they just haven't marketed it enough to convince me.

Kenya – Kenya coffees are some of the finest in the world. They are known as difficult to blend. They have a truly bright flavor that is distinctive. I would say Colombian and Kenyan are the easiest to spot. There's a lot of controversy right now in Kenya about some new botanical growths that some experts are afraid will water down Kenya's richness. I have no doubt that someone will find a way to charge extra, brand the coffee and keep the great Kenyans coming. They're too fine.

Zimbabwe - Zimbabwe coffees share the same basic geography and are up and comers. They can be had at a bargain price because they're unknown. I know a few roasters who label their Zimbabwe coffees "Kenya."

Tanzania – Less well known than Kenyans. More of a bargain. Particularly known for a peaberry, which is a tiny bean. Tiny beans, by the way, are generally better for home roasting.

Brazil – Brazil really has some fine coffees, but they're hard for consumers to find. I've had a Brazil branded as Bandarante that worked great as an espresso. Brazil is a fine example of a country that went corporate. It's had to fight that image. There's a line in an old song that goes, "There's an awful lot of coffee in Brazil". Much of it is rather plain. But, there are a few noteworthy ones so don't fail to try them.

Aged coffees – Aged coffees are coffees that are held for several years in climate-controlled storage. This is all before roasting however. After roasting aged coffees are of no value. Aging was discovered by coffee experts centuries ago who discovered that Java coffees that went the long way around the world (budget freight lines) tasted better. In the days of great blenders, it was typical to add aged coffees to round out a blend. I've had examples of this and they were noteworthy. It is difficult in the current world of quick futures to expect anyone to hang on to a product in order to let it mature. Ellen Reidy, a woman who could taste a different brand of coffee filter, who was a master cupper at Richeimer Coffee, used to produce a Colombian that used both new and aged coffees. What a blend! I've never had another like it.

PARTING ADVICE

Don't get too attached to single varietal coffees. They are the way our 31 Flavors mentality society has grown its market. But there are many great blends as well.

Coffee Gallery

Chapter 3

Roasting: What It Means To You

Pan-American Coffee
Bureau circa 1953

Grandpa dunking donuts.
Some folks frown on it... but
it's a lot of fun

Courtesy of Specialty Coffee Assn. of America

Serving coffee to a guest - after a drawing in an early edition of "Arabian Nights"

Coffee Inspiration

"If bad companions tempt you, don't go along with them." Proverbs 1:10

Why does instant coffee come to mind? But there are others as well. For instance, I've had friends try to get me to enjoy canned coffees. With rare exceptions, the flavor just isn't there. To me, this proverb speaks directly to fads in general. Real coffee enjoyment isn't about going along with the latest trend. In general, I avoid the pack's advice about coffee.

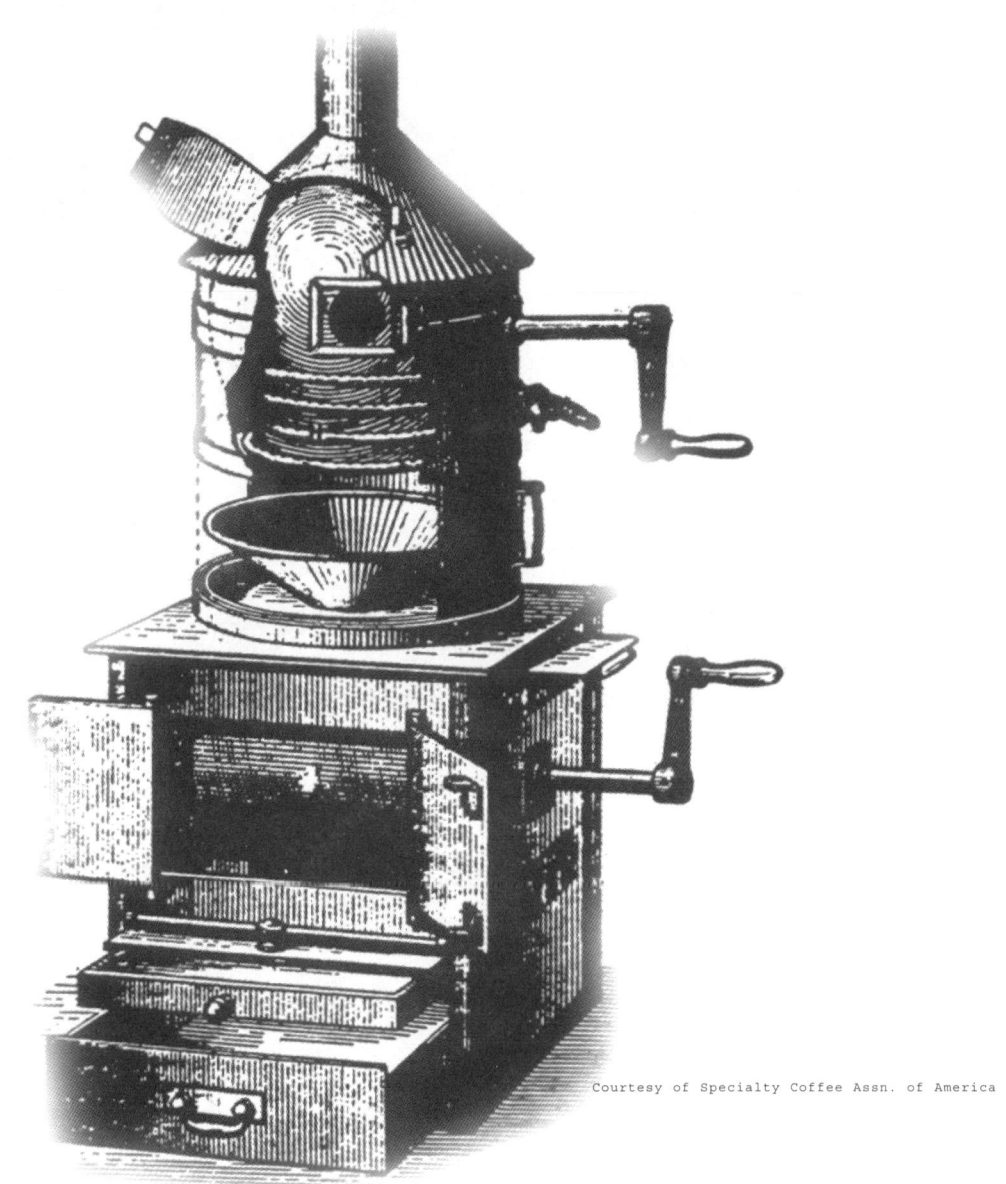

Early French coffee-roasting machine

3

Roasting: What It Means to You

Roasting is best thought of as cooking the beans in preparation to the brewing process. Roasting is where the roaster, or more pretentiously, the roastmaster heats the beans in order to bring forth a certain balance of flavors in advance of your buying the beans and taking them home. The roasting process can accentuate some flavors and even be used to mask others. Roasting can be used to soften a harsh coffee and to brighten a dull one. At its best, roasting is a process used to highlight the best tastes that come from good coffee genes, properly cultivated and processed. Wow, what a mouthful!

I tend to regard roasting as both a craft and an art. When thinking about home roasting it is important to realize that commercial roasters have all sorts of variables that the home roaster does not have. I'll give you an example. Simon Thompson, roastmaster at Craven's Coffee in Spokane, Washington, told me that with certain coffees, he closes down his ventilation exhaust shafts to keep a certain smokiness in the beans. Caribou's Robert Datala has told me he senses a certain point near the end of a roast and he "hits" the roast with a blast of heat in order to bring forth a certain amount of oils. These tricks of the trade are impossible with virtually any home roaster I've yet tried. This does not mean that you should not roast at home. Don't forget that there are roastmasters who use different equipment, some more flexible than others. I know several that use Sivetz roasters, the original "shop" roaster and they produce some beautiful coffees with minimum opportunity to explore options. But, I always want to serve the cause of honesty. Home roasting is like home music recording, another of my passions. There is no way I can compete with the arsenal of audio tricks of any major studio. I do it for my own enjoyment – to satisfy an urge to create. Home roasting is the same. Only you get to drink the results. Practice is the key.

Roasting

Coffees, at least fine ones, are sold and discussed almost exclusively by country of origin. In reality, how and how much a coffee is roasted plays an equal part in how it tastes. Of course if you think of canned commodity coffee, roasting is virtually the same among the major players. Roasting is done simply to cook the beans. Coffees are roasted just enough to bring forth the bright flavor notes and not more because roasting longer causes weight losses.

Specialty coffees are roasted somewhat differently. Every goal in specialty coffee involves taste. Most people have no awareness of how many variables there are in roasting coffee, the different ways to roast and how much effort is being done to improve roasting, or at least understand it.

When you buy a fresh fish, you know there are several ways to cook it. There are similar options in roasting coffee.

Roasting Types

Chances are you've never asked your coffee roaster what style machine he uses to bring the raw beans he buys to perfection in aroma and flavor. There are three basic types of coffee roaster:

DRUM: This is the oldest style. In fact, many upscale 1800s consumers had small drum roasters they would set in their fireplace to roast their own beans. Drums slowly turn the beans over. Drums roast slowly, and practitioners have to be careful not to scorch beans as the drum's bottom is always very hot. Adherents claim the longer roast time creates a deep development of flavors unmatched by other roast technologies. Detractors argue that the long roast times simply reduce acidity (bright flavor). Classic drum roasters have names like Jabez-Burns or Diedrich on them.

CONVECTION DRUM: This variation on the drum roast theme is different because heat efficiency is enhanced using hot air, just like in a home convection oven. This speeds up the roasting process, usually bringing roast times down to the twelve minute range. Since these machines use a combination of direct and indirect heat, there are all kinds of ways to affect the roast. Owners of these machines claim they can produce distinct flavors unmatched by using other technologies. Many companies design and build convection/drum roasters, including Probat, Samiac and W. Roure.

FLUID BED (AIR): Fluid Bed roasters are the modern challengers. While it is sometimes difficult to determine the taste difference between coffee roasted using other technologies, fluid bed results almost always stand out. I often remark to someone that I bet this coffee was done on a Sivetz and I'm usually right. Speaking of Sivetz, the name identifies both a roaster and an historical personality. Michael Sivetz, an New York-born engineer, designed and built the first shop-size air roasters in the 1970s, setting of a revolution in widespread availability of great coffee. Air roasting's strengths are speed and consistency. It is virtually impossible to scorch coffee beans using hot air. Hot air is also unmatched in efficiency, making it possible to roast coffee within eight minutes. Disciples of air roasting believe we have entered a new age of roasting with this method, and will sometimes scoff at older

Italian wrought-iron coffee roaster
Courtesy of Specialty Coffee Assn. of America

technologies as dirty and wasteful. Critics have found a lack of flavor development, a kind-of "brightness over depth" perception in air roasted coffee. I've come to regard it as simply a different option that presents a high resolution flavor profile.

Which is better still comes down to personal preference. When you buy specialty coffee part of what you're buying is the taste buds of the professional who buys and roasts the beans.

Roast Types

Now that you're thoroughly overwhelmed by the available technologies, let's look at the different roast options. Where roaster names and technologies are rarely named even in high end shops, roast profiles are. Words and phrases such as French roast, dark roast, espresso roast have become well known if not understood. I'm going to try to clear this up while not taking sides (not easy for a coffee connoisseur).

CINNAMON ROAST – Lightest of all roasts. Most large chain coffee is cinnamon roast. This is not to say it isn't done in specialty. In fact, there are roasters devoted to light roasts for their best beans, claiming that only the best products can stand up to the revealing nature of light roasts. Very popular in countries where heavy cream works well to smooth out the edges of brightness.

AMERICAN ROAST – A bit of stereotyping because Americans have always had roast diversity (probably get on NPR with that one!) Probably the classic Midwest roast, American roast does seem perfect – no covering up poor coffee by overroasting while developing the richness. What's not to like? Perhaps this is the toughest color to roast because it has the narrowest window of opportunity ... just a little too much and it becomes a French roast. American roast is the only coffee popular straight, without cream or sweetener.

FRENCH ROAST – Virtually unknown in France this is the most often-named roast. It can mean anything darker than American, making it hard to describe in

Roasting: What It Means to You

practical terms. The easiest way to define French roast is whenever the roast is dark enough to reveal the roast and not the coffee aroma. Adherents claim this is full flavor development and they describe it in wine terms indicating a full body.

ESPRESSO ROAST – Means different things to different folks – again. In simplest European terms, espresso roast almost has to be slightly darker roast, there's just something about the high-pressure extraction that tilts the flavor balance to too bright using light roasts. Brands like Illy are virtually American roast, maybe a shade darker. In what has become popularized as a Seattle roast, the coffee is very dark roasted. Adherents claim that it goes better with cream (interesting: cream friendliness is claimed for both dark and light roast coffees) and Italians claim it misses the point of espresso, but it's worth noting that it has resonated with the public.

WEST COAST ROAST – A large West coast roaster likes to claim this roast is the product of clever observation and their willingness to lose profits by roasting away potential weight losses for the sake of total flavor development, the historical truth lies elsewhere. During the 1800s West coast coffee roasters dealt with major shipping and transportation challenges. It was unlikely that any customer would get anything near overnight shipping. Coffee roasters believed that roasting dark to the point where oils

Original hand-signed Sivetz "heat gun" coffee roaster

coated the bean exterior actually created a protective barrier, which prolonged the beans' freshness. Fans of this roast style claim it's the richest and most flavorful of all. Conscientious dark roast objectors say that all the flavor is roast, not coffee, flavor similar to excessive charbroiling. They claim the individual coffee origins cannot be discerned at such a dark roast. Although I personally agree I must admit I've had some swell dark roasted coffees, one in particular, an aged Java was very discernible – I couldn't imagine it better or more distinctive tasting at any other roast.

Coffee Gallery

Chapter Four

Fresh Coffee Checklist

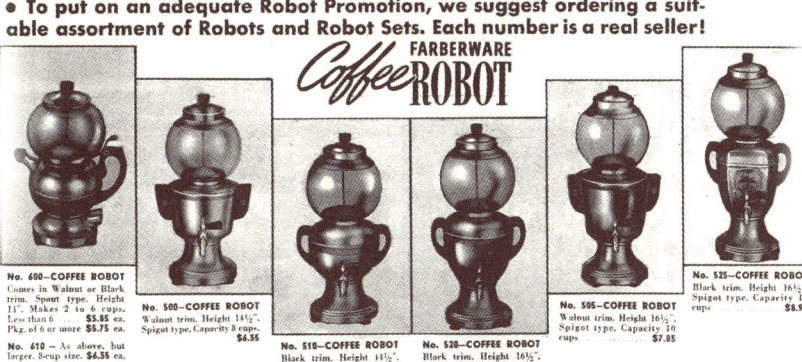

http://www.oldcoffeeroasters.com/robots.htm

The "Enterprise" Pioneer hand stone mill

Courtesy of Specialty Coffee Assn. of America

Coffee Inspiration

"You have been faithful and trustworthy over a little. I will put you in charge of much." Matthew 25:21

This may sound corny, but I really feel a sense of responsibility to the wonderful, beautiful coffees I have received to do my part to bring their goodness forth into the cup, where they really come to life. Like faith, we are handed a gift. Then it's up to us to take the next step to put in into reality in our lives. I return to this analogy often when I'm trying various experiments. It certainly makes the extra labor it takes to get great coffee seem trivial.

4

Fresh Coffee Checklist

You may have visited a wine collector and seen all kinds of bottles, some over a century old, that this hobbyist is saving for the right occasion. Until much progress is made, coffee cannot become a collector's art. Coffee is, like a butterfly, something you must enjoy during its brief lifetime. The ideal window of opportunity for truly fine coffee is from, say six hours after roasting until about ten days later.

Do I honor this fully? Nope. I don't. Every six months or so, my wife Patricia goes through my coffee areas (the whole house) and quizzes me about each sack. There are many leftovers, now stale, that I subconsciously attempted to save.

Does coffee past ten days really taste all that bad? Of course not. This is not an exact science. Actually, it probably is an exact science. What is not exact is the knowledge that would tell you exactly when the coffee will go stale. Unknown factors such as moisture in the bean, moisture in your house, temperatures, oxygen and your own taste buds' discernment are all valid data you would need to know for sure.

In lieu of an exact date, I would do the following:

- Buy relatively small quantities. I need to take my own advice here. It's too easy to see a bunch of great coffees in a sweet smelling shop and want to take them all. Don't.
- If you can use up your coffee within ten days, I'd keep it dry and at room temperature.
- Keep your coffee in the original bag. Fold it over tightly to squeeze out any excess oxygen and use a rubber band to keep it tightly closed.
- If you can't use up your coffee within ten days, throw it in the freezer, not the refrigerator. The freezer does a great job of slowing staling because it removes oxygen and moisture. But, freezing remains controversial. Some coffee experts suspect that once frozen, coffee never returns to its original state. You can't freeze oils, they claim. Others observe the freezing makes the beans overly brittle in grinding. The conservative response is to use freezing only when it is necessary. Why not the refrigerator? Too much moisture.
- Grind your coffee no more than a few hours before you brew. There's actually a theoretical advantage to letting coffee, especially fresh coffee, take a break between grinding and brewing. This prevents any just-released carbon dioxide from causing your coffee to foam up during brewing. When coffee grounds foam up in the brew basket, they're not doing their primary job, which it to soak in hot water and let their oils come forth for you to drink! Overly fresh coffee can actually taste weak for this reason.

ARE CANS A "NO-NO?"

The idea of a can was brilliant, especially when you consider its original purpose – to provide food rations to soldiers in the First World War. The can is actually not a bad idea for coffee storage. What happened is that cans got lighter. Light cans will buckle if the coffee in them releases carbon dioxide. No one buys buckled cans of anything. So, coffee is ground and left to go stale before packaging. There is one exception to the can's bad reputation. Illy, the quite-serious Italian coffee roaster, sells both beans and their preground espresso coffee in cans. Illy is the only manufacturer I know of that can boast that their coffee maintains its freshness in the can. I don't know how they do it. Short of marrying a Rothschild or becoming a Freemason, I know of no way to find out, either, and Illy isn't telling.

Home Roasting

Until the twentieth century, coffee was roasted in the home, often in roasting appliances that utilized the family's fireplace or wood burning stove. In a highly romanticized picture of life, it's easy to imagine the wonderful 19th century wife, humming "When Johnnie Comes Marching Home" while whipping up today's mocha-java. Who knows.

Lately, the coffee industry has experienced an influx of inexpensive home coffee roasters. Obviously, the freshness angle is highly promoted as their reason for being. It's almost undeniable that at some time, the curious coffee lover will want to go all the way and try home roasting.

A few cautions:

- Unlike every other step in the coffee process, roasting does not smell good. I know a professional roaster who regularly throws out his clothes once the roasting smell gets in his blue jeans. Most of the wonderful aroma of coffee is a byproduct of roasting. Most of the bad smells are removed and those are the ones you smell in coffee roasting. My wife Patricia still tells the sad tale of my ruining the house before a dinner party when I tried to show off my manhood by roasting some fresh coffee.
- Fresh roasted coffee must sit before using. Too fresh and you end up with a carbonated beverage in the brew basket. The fantasy sold by home roasting manufacturers is that you'll go straight from the roaster to the brewer. Not so.
- Roasting is an inexact science. I can't believe the amount of superstition and mythology I hear from roasters (like roasting on odd Tuesdays)... no theory is too wild. Home roasters are no

different. The point is that home roasting can easily become obsessive and to date I've never personally produced or experienced results that justify the trouble. I will predict, though, that tomorrow's star roasters are probably today's home roasters, so I should probably keep my mouth shut. Just be sure to open a window.

THE FUTURE

Packaging is where a lot of money is spent in the coffee business. I would predict that in the next few years coffee packaging will improve. The industry knows that its products will become more wine-like (read: expensive) when collectors can save them longer. Wouldn't you like to pull out a very fine 1968 Hills Brothers on Christmas? Okay, how about a 1938 Mocha-Java? That's better.

Coffee Gallery

Chapter Five

All-Time Greatest Coffee Makers

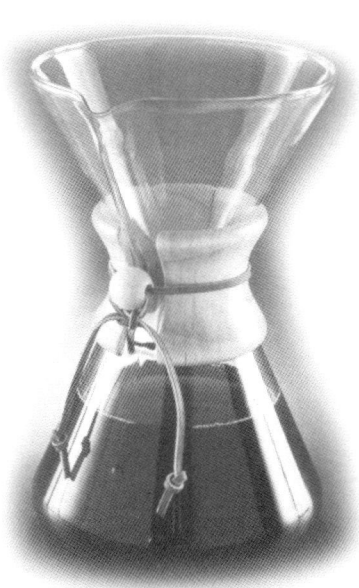

Handblown Chemex Coffee Maker

Found in the permanent collections of the Museum of Modern Art, the Smithsonian, and the Philadelphia Museum of Art.

Coffee Inspiration

"A cheerful disposition is good for your health; gloom and doom leave you bone-tired." Proverbs 17:22

No doubt about it, Proverbs has this one down. Think what a good beverage coffee is: it supplies us with both energy and attitude boosts. I personally believe that God created a world with coffee in it to help energize us. If we follow His other advice about moderation, most of us will profit from coffee.

5

All-Time Greatest Coffee Makers
(or at least they should be famous)

The Chemex story begins with an artist. Peter Schlumbohm, a German immigrant who arrived in America during the last century, didn't even drink coffee. Apparently, he picked it up once he set up shop as a designer. He couldn't find any coffee maker that made coffee to his satisfaction. So, he set to work designing a coffee maker. He decided to go drip method, which makes sense for someone from Germany. He found glass the most appealing material since it adds nothing to the taste. His resulting design is often mistaken as Bauhas-inspired, but Schlumbohm always denied being Bauhas-influenced. What he did was invent a very simple, form and function coffee brewer that has created a cult-like following.

What's unique once you get past the visual appeal?

Chemex uses probably the thickest filter paper in the world. Common wisdom usually has it that less is more filtering-wise. The Chemex filters out any sediment. What results is an ultra-refined brew, yet in my experience it is never weak tasting nor lacking in any flavor, which makes me doubt the less-is-more filter crowd.

Another unorthodox Chemex attribute is it's intentionally lower-than-standard brewing temperature. Now, it's designed for you to pour hot water of your own heating over the grounds. But, Peter Schlumbohm had a long-standing argument with the Coffee Brewing Institute and their insistence the coffee must be brewed at a minimum 195F. Schlumbohm claimed that coffee tasted better when brewed at around 190F. This is still heresy in the coffee world. It says something about the gentility of the times that one of his own competitors (a vacuum maker manufacturer) came forth and defended Schlumbohm against the CBI, saying that the CBI shouldn't mandate such a narrow standard.

Yet another distinction of the Chemex is its use of coarse coffee grounds. Far from obvious, many would assume that such a thick filter paper would work best with fine grinds. In practice, however, the Chemex's thick paper actually slows the drip process, so much so that coarse grounds are best because they don't slow it any further. What results is a rich cup of coffee that many would consider the best they've ever had.

The unusual role of the filter paper in controlling the brewing time makes the Chemex a little more than usually forgiving when it comes to grind. Most drip machines use grind to control the speed at which the water flows though. This means that if you're a little off one way or the other you'll get very weak or very strong (meaning bitter) coffee. The Chemex overcomes this inherent drip limitation to some degree.

The Chemex is one of my favorite coffee makers. It subjectively lacks some of the absolute resolution that only the high temperature/high turbulence vacuum makers extract from your grounds. Honestly, though, the slightly burnished and forgiving ability the Chemex has to seemingly extract just the best flavors is usually in its favor in real world use. I've had coffees that show their flaws under the vacuum maker's magnifier that taste superb when brewed in the Chemex.

CHEMEX "AUTOMATIC" COFFEE MAKER

If you can ever find one of these automatic Chemex coffee makers, grab it!!! It outperforms almost all current coffee makers. True to its roots, it has unique features. For one thing, it has the first-ever temperature control for the hot plate that keeps the coffee warm. Second, and more important, it features a brew interrupt feature that really emulates manual drip, where you pour a little water in and then pause while it drips through before pouring in more, a feature that gives a far richer extraction.

The handblown glass Chemex is a bargain at it's under $100 price. There are machine made units that are nearly as appealing (I can tell the difference but it's not obvious) for around $30. I would call the Chemex a true dessert island choice.

It is, by the way, the easiest of all coffee makers to keep clean and in its original condition.

VACUUM COFFEE MAKER

Vacuum maker
high resolution coffee maker

Courtesy of Specialty Coffee Assn. of America

"Oh, you mean Silex's. Yeah, sure I've heard of them", friend Stuart Daw, of Heritage coffee said when I asked him about Vacuum makers. "Silex brought them to market and from then on the generic name became Silex, just like when someone says "Xeroxes" when they photocopy something."

Apparently my new found love affair with these makers is no fluke.

"They were capable of brewing great coffee," continued Stuart. "They get hot enough, of course and the grounds get nice and soaked." I asked him why they disappeared.

"The Silex was a tricky customer. They required a certain amount of attention. Maybe just a little more than auto-drip but in a restaurant, in the 50s, efficiency was being watched. And the Bunn drips were more reliable."

I told Stuart how I accidentally overflowed the top section once with overzealous boiling.

"I've seen waitresses shoot grounds up to the ceiling. And then, they would try to hurry the return of the brew back into the lower unit by wrapping cold towels around the bottom carafe."

Stuart knows the unit is one of my favorites.

"They're great for a connoisseur," agrees Stuart. "But I don't think you'll see anyone from food service lining up to buy them."

That's alright with me.

BUNN AUTOMATIC DRIP

The Bunn Automatic Drip machine has changed so little that it's hardly recognized for the revolutionary machine it was when it came out. If you're over thirty but under sixty, the Bunn machine is likely the unit that made your first cup of coffee in a restaurant. Bunn, as they say, "owns" the market. Bunn has done this largely through its service network. Bunn uses good decent parts and, like most conservative companies from the Midwestern United States, they change v-e-r-y s-l-o-w-l-y. They're an old fashioned company. I visit them in Springfield, Illinois, every so often. Last time I was there, they were updating their office, from it's 1950s look to, oh, around 1980. The best part is typically Bunn. After getting some design bids, they decided to pitch in "barn-raising" style and complete all the work themselves. The engineer I visited was painting that day.

Bunn is the brainchild of George Bunn. George sat around his kitchen table analyzing a Chemex maker, thinking of ways he could automate it. He wanted to service the restaurant market. Small diners at the time were stuck with vacuum units. It may seem like a golden age to me, but apparently restaurateurs found vacuum makers high maintenance. Anyway, he finally hit upon the right formula. Like all great entrepreneurs, he did more than invent something. He invented a network to support it. Bunn got a reputation for backing up what they sold. They also used (and still do) good parts, constantly working to refine the weak areas. As one of their competitors once put it, "They're so large, they're slow... but they're not stupid."

The Bunn unit was designed using the Chemex-like V-filter. It wasn't until later that they began using their now-famous cupcake design. Many engineers, some of them who work for v-design manufacturers, believe the cupcake design is superior. Bunn also pioneered the shower sprayhead that works to agitate the grounds. They are also known for the fastest brew cycle short of espresso methods... three minutes! Bunn makes a home version of their restaurant brewer. Bunn owners are extremely loyal and steadfast in their belief they own the finest. I have one concern and that is for the unit's always hot water feature. I worry that water kept hot all the time isn't as good as fresh-drawn water for brewing. I must say, though, that I've had some very excellent coffee made in Bunn units. I do know they are serious about coffee.

KITCHENAID 4 CUP DRIP COFFEE MAKER

You may have noticed that this is just one of a few automatic drip coffee makers in this book. Is it the only one that rates? Not really. There are good units from Braun, Capresso, Techni-vorm and I'm sure a few others that escape me.

What sets the KitchenAid apart is is total attention to detail. Unlike virtually any other unit, it does nothing wrong, and a few things right exclusively.

Classic KichenAid grinder - my dream is to bring it back!

For instance, most autodrip coffee makers just don't meet the minimum temperature standards, not by a long shot. I once measured a Krups unit that barely reached 180 during its brew cycle. The KitchenAid hits 195 almost instantly, and stays there for the duration.

Most autodrip coffee makers fail to get all the grounds wet. It's like when I ask my son to water our lawn – some parts get submerged and others remain dry as a bone. When this happens in a coffee maker, it means that you just wasted any dry grounds, and the ones that got wet probably gave more flavor than they should, which adds bitterness. The KitchenAid gets all the grounds wet, but none more that the others. It's the best I've tested.

Most autodrip coffee makers take too long to brew. Those little heaters just chug along, but they end up taking ten minutes or more to brew. That's just too long to extract from the grounds. Of course, there is no right or wrong on this. The Europeans demand a little more bitterness from their coffee. The KitchenAid gets it right in America, at just a six minute brew.

I wish I could say I own KitchenAid stock but I don't. I honestly like the unit. The fact that it is around forty dollars and widely available probably lessens its snob appeal, but so be it. There are other books for snobs to read. This one is aimed at great coffee, pure and simple.

Now, I hear some folks saying, "wait a minute, Kevin. The KitchenAid only brews four cups. That's cheating." I know. My question back is how much coffee do you drink? The KitchenAid brews four cups, in reality it brews two good-sized mugs. This is about the perfect amount for two commuters getting ready to leave for work in the morning. Yes, I'm sure that the Kitchen Aid is more easily able to brew in six minutes because the water volume is less.

And, before you mistake me for a Kitchen Aid employee remember that there are other units that are good.

HOW TO MAKE PERFECT COFFEE WITH THE KITCHENAID 4-CUP

First, fill up the carafe with pure water. I use my own town's municipal well water, but I run it through a Sears R/O filter. Some coffee purists object to r/o water, saying it's too "dead" but I find it works fine. It's not true that it removes so many minerals that you're drinking distilled water. You're drinking mineral water that only contains dissolved minerals. Autodrip makers are prone to "liming" or calcium buildup. R/O water adds so little calcium that this is less of a problem. Consider R/O for home espresso machines as well.

Meanwhile, the KitchenAid works best with around thirty-six grams of medium-fine ground coffee. That's around nine grams per cup, slightly less than regulation, but likely far more than you're using right now if you've been following the canned coffee manufacturer's suggestions. The combination of a short brew cycle and a higher amount of ground coffee produces the very rich but not-bitter coffee that you'll enjoy.

I have used several filters. The Melitta #4 and Green Mountain #4 filters work equally well. Other than that, this unit is truly automatic. There's very little in the

All-Time Great Coffee Makers

The French Press
My neighbor Diana likes it better than I do.
Photo of the Cafe Americaine WFP set.

way of tweaking that I need to recommend. For job security, my over-the-top recommendation may be unwise. So be it.

It's a great coffee maker.

FRENCH PRESS

The French press is not one of my favorite coffee makers, but its popularity is strong enough that it deserves mention, if not my sincere affection. Basically, the press is simplicity itself, and ingenious in its design. The idea is to throw some grounds into a glass container. Then, hot water is poured in on top of the grounds. Stir briefly, to facilitate extraction. After a few minutes, a screened plunger top is inserted, the plunger is pressed down, pushing all the grounds to the pot's bottom. Then hot coffee is poured from the press, having already been filtered.

The Press is cheap to produce, its looks are easy on the eyes.

Sounds great doesn't it?

I find a number of problems with the press. First of all, the press' pot section must be scalded with hot water just before coffee grounds are tossed in, an extra step that, if you forgo it, the coffee will likely be too cool.

Second, the grounds must be coarsely ground. How coarsely? You just have to experiment. The way to tell is to keep grinding finer until one time, when you press the top down, it won't budge about halfway through the process.

Third, the press coffee can't be stirred with the top down. Therefore, when pouring multiple cups, each person gets one that's different in strength.

Fourth, the press grounds may be compacted in the pot's bottom, but they aren't exactly out of the way. If you have one cup from the press and pour a second a few minutes later, the second cup may well be overextracted as the water continues to interact with the grounds.

Fifth, the press is hard to clean. I find the screen must be disassembled each time or coffee oils and trapped sediment will accumulate and add off-tastes and bitterness.

After all I've said, you'd think the press would be a dismal failure. It's not. It's got legions of fans, who probably would nod at most of what I've said, but they'd say they love it anyway.

I will say that the press is a system that is quite popular among those who cup (evaluate) coffee. I believe it is because the press closely emulates the method used of steeping coffee in sampling it.

Australian inventor (and close personal friend) Ian Bersten tried to market a press with a second robotic arm that would both agitate the extraction and homogenize the strength during brewing. It was a resounding failure in the market but is worth seeking through the worldwide web. It really makes the best press coffee I've ever had.

Coffee Gallery

Chapter Six

BREWING (THE MOST IMPORTANT PART)

The standard for great auto drip making—solid midwestern styling. The Bunn Pour-omatic home model B-8 coffee brewer is still a classic.

Coffee Inspiration

"It is more blessed to give than to receive" – Acts 20:35

I have to admit, I sometimes have felt at a loss when it comes to giving to others in casual ways. I don't build, so my contributions to helping my neighbor build his new addition are out. I have spent times with little money to give, but one of the joys of any coffee connoisseur is to give pleasure, even the pleasure of a single cup of excellent coffee.

Zassenhaus Perfect Home Grinder

6

GRINDING: A Great Place to Start

Grinding is probably the most important factor in making coffee and it gets the least attention. Years ago the coffee grinder was at the center of most kitchens. Following World War II the food canning industry sold both the major coffee roasters and then consumers the idea that food of all kinds could be preserved intact using cans. Lately, savvy consumers have returned to fresh ground coffee as they have fresh vegetables and other foods. The best place to store your coffee flavors is in the bean. Owning a grinder means you get to keep that flavor intact until just before you brew.

WHY GRIND COFFEE AT ALL

A good analogy to the need to grind is a stir fry. When you stir fry a vegetable you cut them in smaller pieces. Why? Well, it gets the heat evenly into the pieces. It's also a good analogy because you want to cut the pieces into even sizes.

It's the same for coffee. If you take some whole coffee beans and run hot water over them, you'll find that the results are somewhat weak. Grinding coffee beans serves two purposes: First, cutting coffee beans into smaller pieces makes it easier for the water to reach the flavor oils in a short period of time. Second, when making drip coffee ground coffee actually controls the speed at which the water travels through the filter. So, it's doubly important for coffee to be ground consistently and to the right fineness.

Grinder Types

Basically, there are two types of coffee grinders: Spinning blade "choppers" and mills. The blade versions continuously slice the beans while you press a button on top. Mills actually smash the beans between two metal wheels.

BLADE GRINDERS

The advantage of the blade types is they are cheap to manufacture and free from alignment. It's simple to use one – you just fill the upper hopper with beans, pop on the lid and press. You'll hear a whir as well as the sound of the beans being cut. The method of controlling grind fineness is timing. By design you are supposed to press the button and count by watch or a clock. Some manufacturers even provide simple guides (ten seconds for drip, etc.) But the timing method has been shown to be unreliable. Consistency is another drawback of this method. Positioned on a countertop, the blade chopper cannot evenly divide the beans. There is no good method to place each bean in the blade's path so that each bean is equally divided. Blade type users often end up shaking the units while in operation in order to try to influence the equal cutting of all the beans. In practice this is very difficult to accomplish. Blade grinders produce a notoriously uneven grind. To a casual user or to someone who uses very fine grind - forgiving methods such as a French press the blade grinder may be satisfactory. But, drip brewers depend upon consistently ground coffee to control brewing contact time. Also, blade grinders work using tiny motors that heat up quickly and transmit the heat into the grinding chamber. That heat uses up precious coffee flavors that you really want to keep until you brew.

Grinding: A Great Place to Start

MILLS

Mills are preferred by experts because they grind more consistently and they allow the user to adjust the overall fineness of the grind. If you've ever seen a mill used for flour you have a pretty good idea how they work. The idea of a mill is to crush the coffee beans between two metal burrs. There is an adjustment for the user to cause the burrs to get closer in order to control the amount of fineness. Mills aren't exactly perfect at delivering consistently sized grounds but they're much better than blades. Metal mill burrs aren't prone to heating up. Supermarket coffee grinders are mills. A hundred years ago, manual coffee grinders were made that featured large wagon wheels. Turning these wheels caused the grinder to function. These grinders are popular as antiques today and sell for high prices at auctions. If they have been maintained they will perform very well as coffee grinders. The biggest disadvantage of mill grinders is cost. It simply costs more to produce a grinding mechanism than a spinning blade. The other possible disadvantage is that every mill design must be optimized for a range of grinds. Some mills are best suited for drip coffee and cannot grind finely enough for espresso. Others may work well for espresso but fail to produce a consistent coarse grind for drip. But, this drawback is not important to most consumers who make coffee using the same unit each day. For them it is just important to obtain a good reliable grinder that can grind fresh coffee consistently for their brewer.

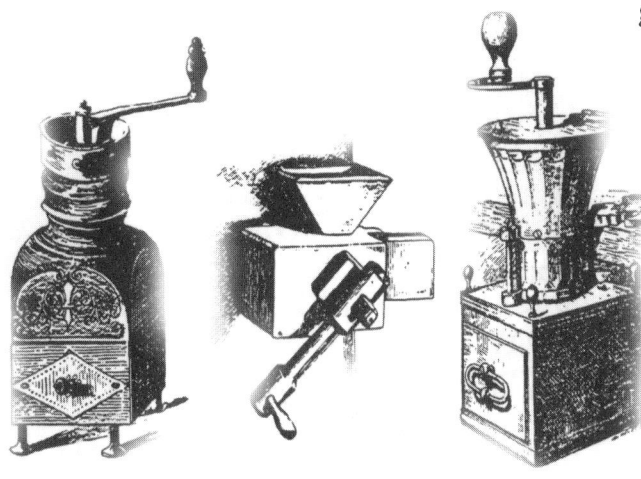

Early french wall & table grinders

Courtesy of Specialty Coffee Assn. of America

GRIND SUGGESTIONS

Both coffee brewer and grinder manufacturers have been guilty of buck passing when it comes to making good recommendations about grinding. In order to get perfect coffee it is necessary that you do some tests using your brewer in order to get the right grind. Be sure you use two tablespoons of ground coffee per six-ounce cup. In watching people make coffee in their homes I've found that most people use too little ground coffee and grind too fine. One reason they complain about too-strong coffee is that their coffee is bitter, which happens whenever you combine too few grounds and overgrind them.

Here are some examples of different coffee making methods and how to grind to get best results:

Manual Drip (cone style) - These are usually made of plastic and sell for a few dollars, yet they can make great coffee. Use a fine grind, because they use a small amount of coffee and so water travels through fast. A fine grind means four minutes contact time.

Automatic Drip (Mr. Coffee/Bunn) - These are easy to spot because the filters are flat on the bottom like a cupcake. Flat-bottomed units tend to extract quite quickly, often in four minutes. Therefore, they work best using medium fine grinds. If brewing extends to more than five minutes, back off to a coarser grind.

Automatic Drip (Melitta/cone) – This unit uses a more pointed bottom, which tends to prolong the brewing time. Ironically, the European developers of this method also favor stronger, more bitter coffee and tend to also recommend finer grinds. Manufacturers usually compensate by brewing at lower temperatures. My suggestion: Start with medium fine grind and then go coarser if your coffee is too strong.

Grinding: A Great Place to Start

Vacuum Method - The vacuum coffee maker uses a flame (or stovetop) to heat water which shoots up into a second bowl for brewing. Since the user controls the contact time the grind is variable. Usually, the grind is very fine, almost espresso and the contact time is very short, often three to four minutes.

French Press – This method requires a coarse grind. If you grind fine, you'll end up with fine grounds in your cup and the "press" can get stuck when you attempt to push it down. Five to seven minutes is a reasonable contact time range. If coffee is too weak, then grind finer but not too fine.

Espresso – Commercial espresso machines require their own grinders. Espresso is in fact a hypersensitive drip method that extracts using a twenty-second contact time. Such short contact times require more precision and the grinder burrs need to be optimized accordingly. Some consumer machines are more forgiving. Designers have worked to develop technologies that share the pressure duties between the grind and other mechanisms. Such machines generally include special notices that inform you to use somewhat coarser grinds. In that case use a very fine grind, close to the vacuum.

Which is the right grind? Answer: Depends upon your coffee maker. Tip: Most consumers err on grinding too fine.

WATER QUALITY

I was standing in the test kitchen of one of the top coffee roasters in the U.S. We had previously attended the first roast of a precious blend he had concocted the night before and were about to brew for the first time. Anticipation was mounting as I was preparing to toast the success of this new blend. Since it was his blend and his ego, I stood back as he prepared the brew. Ten grams of beans were scooped up from the still-near-warm bag of beans he'd hand carried from the roasting plant. The correct grind

Great Coffee

was dialed in on the Ditting grinder. At my request, he brewed in the Techni-Vorm coffee maker.

Like many successful people, he thrives on an urban business setting but has long ago fled the city for a more pastoral country setting in which to live. Here on a farmette, this roaster can drink the rewards of a life well-spent in roasting great coffee.

Only one problem. His 1870 farm house draws water from a shallow well that pumps up water that I nearly mistook for already-brewed weak Hills Brothers coffee. "Nearly", because the aroma was hardly coffee-like and instead put forth the aroma of iron and sulfur, two apparently inert but unattractive "nose notes".

In horror, I watched as this great roaster simply turned on the faucet and began filling the water reservoir of the Techni-Vorm. "Doesn't that bother you?", I asked with considerable restraint as the clear holding tank of the coffee maker turned a warm orange-ish color.

"My coffee will taste through", the roaster said smugly.

How do you like that? Coffee, even as strong as I make it, is something like 98% water. To me, hearing my friend tell me this would be like hearing Dr. Christian Barnard admitting he doesn't wash his hands before doing a heart transplant. "After all", he would say, "the patient must take antibiotics anyway".

So what about water?

Water has a specific job in the coffee making process. Think of water like a railway train that travels between the coffee water tank and the coffee serving pot. On its journey, the water (railway) must stop and pick up flavors waiting in the coffee ground particles (railway station).

With me so far? Now, keeping the railway analogy, minerals in the water are like passengers already on the train. Meaning that highly mineraled water will accept less coffee flavor during the time it is mixing with the coffee ground particles. Therefore, less flavor.

Coffee formulas, including measurements, ground fineness, even water brewing temperature have been determined based upon tests using water with a proper mineral balance, just as a railroad must determine the passenger load and attach the correct number of cars to carry the number of passengers they anticipate.

Brewing, the Most Important Part

The good news is, unlike railroads, we coffee aficionados know in advance the number of flavor passengers we wish to pick up on our route to brewing perfection. We want to absorb (or pick up) enough coffee particles so that our finished brew is approximately 2% coffee to 98% water. If we use water that is already saturated with particles such as iron or sulfur, we will brew weak coffee because less coffee will have been absorbed.

Other factors are important. Oxygen actually helps to stimulate extraction, something fresh tap water contains aplenty. Water that is distilled, boiled for too long or has been sitting idle for weeks in a plastic jug is likely to be deficient of fresh oxygen.

Artificially softened water has problems, too. For one thing, the way all water softeners work is by exchanging particles of, say calcium, for one of sodium. This is good news for bathing or doing the laundry, because sodium helps your soaps cleanse and the rinse water to remove them, whereas calcium deposits a film and prevents the soaps from dissolving. But, in coffee making, the sodium throws a major wrench in the process. Tales of tragedy using softened water to brew coffee abound. There are actual case histories telling of brew baskets with paper filters that became clogged during extraction, halting the process.

No coffee. No fun.

So, what does one do as far as water is concerned?

First, if your city water has a good reputation for health, I say use it as opposed to bottled water. You'll save money. You benefit from its being chock full of oxygen. Is there too much chlorine, adding a sour flavor note to your brew? You can always draw the water in advance of brewing by twenty minutes or so. The chlorine will evaporate as will some of the oxygen, so there is some potential trade-off. Another solution is to get a water filter unit (such as the Everpure) that uses activated charcoal to remove the chlorine as well as some other minor pollutants. These are fine for city water lines, although none is sufficient for well water unless you also get a private chlorinator to first remove bacteria. My family suffered acute infections from drinking water from a private well treated with a Multi-Pure unit. The salesperson who sold it to me was totally unaware of the need to first chlorinate all drinking water. Buyer beware.

In fact, if you drink well water, or your tap water is drawn through lead pipes or from government sources you can't trust, I am going to risk generalities and suggest buying bottled water. Although *Consumer Reports* (in yet another of their mock-socialist panic attacks on water bottlers) claims water bottling companies need only meet minimal tap water standards, the truth is that the profit incentive has forced water bottlers to publish in-depth reports proving the quality of their water well in excess of minimum federal standards.

Brand preferences aside, there are three basic types of bottled water suitable for use in coffee brewing.

SPRING WATER - The name implies the use of springs from which the wonderful water must be from. What's going on here? Well, somewhere, probably 50 miles or so from the downtown or industrial center of any major city there are still clean water springs. The best are located underground so air pollutants won't get in during rainfall. Spring water is generally acknowledged to be the favorite brewing water for coffee, because it typically contains a mild amount of minerals, in a natural state.

ARTESIAN WELL WATER - Artesian wells are underground wells that may be deeper than springs. The implied benefits are that the water may indeed be better protected from evils of man's industry. The implied drawback is that many water problems are not man-made but natural (naturally occurring radium is typical of deep well water). Also, artesian wells often have very high mineral levels (often healthful) that can interfere with balanced coffee extractions (I assume we don't need to repeat the railway analogy). So artesian well water is not a coffee brewing favorite.

DRINKING WATER - What do you do in the age of technology when you own a big water bottling plant in the middle of a great big superfund site? Why, make your market the cleanup of maybe questionable nearby lake water by first distilling it to remove all the bad minerals (and good ones as well) and then scientifically add some back in order to make it taste and look better than distilled. Does it work for coffee? The answer is a qualified "yes". Here's the good news: **DRINKING** water is arguably the most consistent from brand to brand, practically guaranteeing consistent results. The process "levels the playing field" as corporate executives are inclined to say. It is the closest thing to "drinking water from concentrate" that you can find. It is also the most easy to obtain (the office water cooler standard issue) and price-friendly of bottled waters. Since the mineral balance is restored artificially, the mineral balance is generally on the low side, ensuring a good, strong healthy extraction (the train arrives at the coffee grounds' depot practically with plenty of empty seats, if you know what I mean).

The down side is: DRINKING water seems to lack some of the subjective natural tastes that the best spring waters have. Whether this affects coffee is one of the best after-hours arguments at the Specialty Coffee Association's conventions. My own philosophy is that any difference that can be tasted by itself (in a dixie cup of plain water, for instance) will affect to a greater or lesser degree the final cup.

CONCLUSION

As someone who brews ten half gallon pots of coffee to "try out" a commercial brewer in an afternoon, I consider the cost to be a more important factor than for readers.

Also, in this world of coffee subjectivity where so little can be duplicated, I still wish to standardize these experiments so readers can expect similar results when they try them at home. Therefore, I use three brands of drinking water for virtually all published tastings. On a rare occasion (Christmas or my birthday) I will spring for spring water.

Were I to test in an area where decent tap water were available, I would carbon filter and use it without hesitation.

One helpful hint: Since bottled waters are invariably stale, lacking the inborn oxygen advantages of freshly drawn tap water, the best way to at least partially breathe life into your water is to briskly shake the water jug before pouring. Should you have a water cooler, simply stir crazily after drawing.

FILTERING COFFEE

Nowhere in brewing do the old "spouse" tales come out like they do in the area of filtering. Filtering coffee is necessary unless you drink the grounds. Don't laugh, in the Middle East, they do. But, most of the world drinks some form of filtered coffee. Actually, most of the world drinks some form of filtered drip. Even espresso is a filtered drip method.

The choices of filters are listed as follows:

Paper – By far the most common U.S. method. It was unknown until Frau Melitta Benz decided to try it, at least that's what she's known for. Paper is relatively cheap, relatively taste-free, and very easy to clean up. The main choice has become whether or not to use bleached white paper or non-bleached or brown paper. I believe the brown paper has slightly more of its own taste and therefore I prefer white paper.

Metal – You can't miss the widespread promotion of gold filters. Many vacuum makers in the 1950s used stainless steel filters. Stainless steel or gold, the results are similar. They are pretty inert, taste-wise. They must be cleaned. I personally find that gold filters filter a little less than I'd like in drip makers, but it's a choice I could live with. Cleanup is a little more difficult. The French press uses a filter that is both difficult to clean and even requires a coarser grind in order that it "press" the coffee to the pot's bottom easily (see French press). With any metal filter, I would flush the grounds down the sink and sponge the filter off right after brewing to keep it fresh. Once in a blue moon, I'd sponge it with baking soda just to remove any possible buildup of coffee oils. The claimed environmental savings of using reusable metal filters instead of disposable paper is probably offset by the extra water you use to clean them.

Glass – Some vacuum makers (current Cona, antique Silex) use a removable glass filter rod. The rod has bumps on it that actually provide enough space for coffee to flow around but not grounds. It's so ingenious, I had to mention it. No one's using them except the latest Cona vacuum maker. They clean easily but they do break. Glass is the best of all materials in its ability to add no taste of its own and its ability to wipe clean.

Cloth – Only the Hario vacuum maker is currently using cloth filters. Cloth filters used to be the standard of excellence, but they have one very bad tendency – they can pick up coffee oils. Cloth filters are typically stored in a glass of water between brewings. If you don't change the water frequently they can become moldy as well. Cloth is a very good method of filtering, it seems to work to allow just the right amount of oils through with little sediment. There's a line of hemp filters out of (where else?) California made by Mr. Natural. Good as they are as filters, I find they add a taste of their own, which the purist will likely find unacceptable. Be aware that the grind you find works for paper filters may be different than the one you need if you switch to cloth or metal. The porosity (hole size) varies and therefore so does the flow rate. For instance, if you grind medium for a paper filter, you may find you need to grind finer for a cloth one in order to slow down the flow. This applies to drip only, since it is the one method that uses the filter as a flow regulator. French presses all use a coarse grind to prevent the filter from getting stuck as you "press" it. The vacuum sucks well enough to overpower whatever grind you use, especially since the grounds are loosely floating around during most of the filtering stage.

Espresso machines use their own built-in metal filter. This filter must be kept in pristine condition. Most machine manufacturers recommend abrasive cleaners to remove coffee oils.

Courtesy of Specialty Coffee Assn. of America

Cafetan
Oriental coffee house keeper's costume

Coffee Gallery

Chapter Seven

Great Coffee Out (Cafe Away)

Upscale coffee shop with roaster in background

Courtesy of Specialty Coffee Assn. of America

A coffee house in the time of Charles II

Coffee Inspiration

"But godliness with contentment is great gain." I Timothy 6:6

Coffee is no substitute for a relationship with God. My own obsession with coffee is always well beneath a true spiritual relationship. To miss this would be akin to being a television reviewer and not realizing the difference between a T.V. screen and a real life person. However, coffee sure adds that extra notch of contentment. Given coffee's paradoxical ability to stimulate and to relax simultaneously, it's really an ideal accompaniment to reflection. I once suggested cup holders in the pews to my pastor. He broke out in a hearty laugh, while the elders on the council gave me their best raised eyebrows. I'm not sure I was kidding.

Mad dog in a coffee house - caricature by Rowlandson

Courtesy of Specialty Coffee Assn. of America

7

CAFE AWAY (or Great Coffee Out)

I want to start by telling you that the best coffee you will ever have once you've read this book is the coffee you make at home. However, there is good coffee out and ways to spot it.

First, ask when the coffee was made. My rule of thumb is to never drink coffee that is more than one hour old. There are devices called airpots that are large thermoses. These have been marketed as better to keep coffee fresh and piping hot. I can vouch for the latter. I once tested one. I left it overnight and scalded my hand the next morning as I poured the coffee down the drain. Efficient it was. The advantage of airpots is they reduce oxygen getting to the coffee, which reduces staling. Airpots also are supposedly less harsh than setting an open carafe on a hot plate. The hot spot that can burn the coffee is spread out using an airpot, but there is no way that it eliminates the effects of heat on the coffee. That is naïve. Airpot or not, the freshness of coffee is best within an hour of brewing.

I look for places that grind the coffee. It isn't always a guarantee, but it indicates a commitment to coffee because it is labor intensive.

Restaurants left fine coffee years ago. I happen to live in Chicago. One of our best known restaurants is Charlie Trotters. He's always getting national press. Charlie's coffee is lousy in my opinion. Chefs simply do not take ownership for coffee. In my opinion, this will remain until chefs make the coffee in their kitchens. Putting coffee at wait stations throughout the restaurant is a sure-fire way of keeping coffee mediocre.

Given the choice of a Starbucks or Dunkin' Donuts, I will always take the Dunkin' Donuts. Starbucks burns their beans. Dunkin' Donuts doesn't.

Great Coffee

Once in a great while, a restaurant still has an urn. An urn is a giant coffee maker that brews a gallon of coffee using a pound of grounds. The best urns use cloth filters. Done correctly, the urn is the one method of coffee making out that can produce better coffee than you or I can at home, for reasons that can keep coffee aficionados arguing all night. Urns have all but disappeared, but there are rare moments in life where you may still find them. It is a dream of mine to own one some day and to use it on occasion. I'm sure I'd make a lot of friends who'd come by to help me drink all the coffee.

Coffee Gallery

Chapter Eight

Coffee Collecting:
A visit to a coffee auction

It looks grand
Tell you the truth, today's $50 auto drip makers brew better coffee. But this one sure looks great when company drops by.

Coffee Inspiration

"The fool hath said in his heart, 'There is no God.'" Psalm 53:1

I have a friend I describe as a devout atheist. I truly thank God that I know him. I feel very sorry for my friend, who is otherwise a good man and I still occasionally pray that he is someday given the gift of faith. In the inevitable arguments my friend and I have held over the years (always accompanied by great coffee) I have often observed that he is looking for some great revelation as a sign. Personally, it's the little things that most often reinforce my own faith. I recently held my baby niece Kathleen in my arms and she gave me a smile, the first one ever according to her very wise mother. I ran out of gas two weeks ago in one of my city's worst neighborhoods. A very poor but wonderful man gave me ride and even lent me a gas can. This is evidence of a greater power, and a benevolent one. When I sit outside on a beautiful summer morning, cup with steam pouring from it in my hand, and taste the rich volcanic oils extracted moments before, can I doubt God's hand in the process?

The Trophy
and the winner is...

These coffee makers all look like trophies, but for
award-winning coffee, they're losers

8

COFFEE COLLECTING: A VISIT TO A COFFEE AUCTION

"Art is dead", exclaimed art critic/performance artist Marcelle DuChamp upon reviewing an airplane propeller close-up for the first time in 1934.

"There is no way painting can compete with this", was his final proclamation.

While I'm not ready to toss out my favorite objects 'd Art to collect only assorted industrial designs, I will admit to a certain fascination with inventions of the machine age.

While conventional artwork adorns the walls, or takes up space in an otherwise vacant corner, machines look cool and do things. Some of the best designed coffee gear is beyond function in its appeal, at least I think so.

Apparently so do others, all gathered together under a canvas tent to outbid each other on some of the treasures sold from the recently closed John Conti museum, in Louisville, Kentucky.

So it was, that Patricia Gibbons and I flew in for a visit and the possibility of finding some new acquisitions for our growing collection.

Like all great artwork, great industrial designs tell a story, the development and refinement of human invention. For this reason, as much as I detest certain aspects of shopping malls, for example, they are, in effect, modern art museums. Often, their "exhibits" are a better reflection of the life and times of our modern world than the so-called modern art museums, which often appear to me as out of touch embittered mausoleums for the rich, demonstrating only how remote the aristocrat has become from their previous leadership roles. Of course, to deny the rich their role in defining the shopping mall would be in itself a great mistake.

Anyway, back to Louisville. John Conti, Louisville's premier local roaster, amassed quite a collection over the past 17 years, which had been until this year displayed mostly in a museum open to the public. Although well attended, Conti, probably realizing he had at least one of everything, decided to call it quits, keep a few choice items and allow his booming wholesale coffee business take up the museum space.

Auctions such as this are as close as most collectors can get to a Las Vegas-style adrenaline rush, with an energy to all this that I found quite appealing. Probably luck that I forgot my checkbook.

First, the most surprising thing to me is that old coffee tins do very well in commanding respectable or perhaps the word is "outrageous" prices. Save your old Maxwell House cans. Or is it just nostalgia for the time when these brands were still quality names, which means any

Appliance manufacturers in the 1800s were always adding little styling changes to reclaim their market share

Coffee Collecting

I Dream of Genie

If you rub these coffee makers together does great coffee come out? The answer: Probably not.

can after 1975 is likely worthless. For what it's worth, I saw Saturday morning sales of 1940s Folgers coffee cans starting at $70. All I know is I was saving my cash for more interesting stuff.

I was glad I did because soon the bidding moved on to some classic coffee grinders. Those who think latest is always greatest will be surprised when I tell you that coffee grinders were better fifty years ago. Hobart and others built grinders for shops that did a better job on the grinds most customers used then (and still do). The fact that they were so well built is in evidence by the number of them still in existence, and for this reason, they are the bargains of collectors. I was able to pick up a 1920s Hobart for just $40. As expected, the unit performed perfect grinds, with no adjustment the moment I got it home.

I picked up another less-well-known grinder for $12. The ultimate slap in the face of new technology came when the auctioneers raffled off an almost-new Ditting Swiss grinder (current new retail: $1,200) for five dollars. It was a surreal moment, but I have to remember that I was among collectors and, in fairness to the Ditting, it isn't bad (although is does nothing to unseat the Hobart) it's just not rare or old.

Many of the auction's participants were members of the Mill Association, a collectors' group dedicated to old grinders. One of its members told me that he doesn't even drink coffee, after I asked him which grinder he thought did the most even grind. I still can't quite understand what possessed him to become obsessed with grinders for a product he doesn't consume, but, I will say that this group added a strong presence to the ceremonies. There were others who were also coffee connoisseurs and our discussions were lively and fruitful. It was nice to discover that there were others outside the few I know, who realize the value of these products.

Sleek, modern lines creep into these early 20th Century coffee maker designs

This report would be remiss if it did not highlight the presence of Ed Kvetko, former CEO/co-owner of Gloria Jean's Coffees. Kvetko, who long ago told me of his dream of establishing his own coffee museum, was there (along with Gloria Jean herself) and his now-endless supply of money, which on at least one occasion, he used to outbid me.

It became first unusual, then irritating, and ultimately humorous to hear the auctioneer's gavel pound the table, followed by "number five", Ed's bid number. After awhile, members of the audience, having no recourse since they were constantly being outbid, began chanting Ed's number in unison in synch with the auctioneer. Whereas I and others needed to raise our hands to grab attention of our bids, "Number 5", never out of the interest of the auctioneer, was able to take home all kinds of objects by the slightest raise of his eyebrows to signal interest. Ed's body language was the only clue one had as to the possibility of outbidding him. At times, when an object would obviously only serve as backup for one already in his possession, Kevtko would sit relaxed in his chair and conveniently stop bidding at just over $20, allowing the middle class participants an opportunity to pick up this or that knickknack.

Other times, however, Ed would move forward on the edge of his seat, at rapt attention, and immediately outbid even the bravest of competitors. Considering that I know Ed has been around the world on similar expeditions, I can't wait to see his final museum, which he told me he's locating near his house in Fort Myers, Florida.

After finally outbidding "number five" on a Michael Sivetz-designed (and signed) home roaster, I finally relaxed, only to enter an accidental bidding war with Patricia. Although she was sitting immediately to my right, we became confused during a bid for a 1970s KitchenAid consumer grinder. Knowing how much I wanted it, Patricia entered a bid, which I heard but did not realize she had made. In the tension and confusion, I raised the bid, to the surprise of the auctioneer, who knew we were together, although he realized a good thing when he saw it, and snapped his gavel to close the sale. I glanced over at Kvetko, who smirked.

Now I know why Gloria Jean kept silent the whole time.

Coffee Gallery

Chapter Nine

Espresso History and Drinks

Pan-American Coffee
Bureau circa 1953

Good things happen over coffee

9

ESPRESSO HISTORY

There are many different versions of exactly how the espresso was invented. Even the name has multiple origins. Does it mean express as in Federal Express or fast? Does it mean "expressly for you" as in one cup for one customer? Or does it refer to expressing or squeezing every bit of flavor from the bean? So many different inventors put so many ideas into the espresso we enjoy today that trying to find one or two "fathers" of espresso has become pointless.

If it were an American development with so many creators, we might never have gotten it to market as we would probably still be in court trying to assign portions of credit to the various contributors.

It is fair to say that the Italians as a nation have embraced espresso as their national drink since its invention nearly 100 years ago. It is also fair to say the cappuccino and latté are what have traveled to our shores in popularity.

Although Senior Pavoni did not invent the espresso machine, he is credited with adding an important steam release valve to his model and for a Steve Jobs-like marketing of the espresso during the early 1900s.

Many American connoisseurs of coffee rightly point out that Italians may well have invented espresso as a means of getting all the flavor possible from mediocre coffee beans they tend to purchase on the world market. However, those doubters, including me, are happily surprised when they finally taste espresso brewed from the best-quality arabica coffees, just slightly dark-roasted. Fault or virtue, all espresso machines tend towards presenting a harshness in the high end flavor notes rather than the subtle sweetness that, say, a Chemex will provide when both brew the best lighter-roast coffees.

ESPRESSO DRINKS

Commercial Espresso Machine - lots of parts like a sports car

Espresso has become popular as a drink, more often as a drink base. It's easy to understand the various drinks but there's little standardization, either country to country or from coffee bar to coffee bar.

Mass commercial coffee companies have made it even more confusing by labeling powdered mixed drinks with espresso sounding names.

Let's begin by clearing the air about espresso. Espresso is coffee that is made under power. If you look under the hood of your automatic drip machine you'll see that gravity pulls the water down over the ground coffee and it simply leaves as coffee down below under its own weight. Not true for espresso. Water is shot under very high pressure through the grounds. One thing to remember: There are hundreds of tiny flavors that make up coffee of any kind. Dramatically speeding up the brewing process alters the flavor balance in espresso. Yes, it's still coffee but it is also its own drink. It is so different that the coffee industry treats it separately. Not only the brewing machines but the bean varieties, roasts and grinders are specified differently for espresso and espresso drinks.

Espresso History

Espresso was invented as a way to give everyone their own drink. Italy was the place, the early 1900s the time. There's some disagreement about who did what but there's no disagreement that several inventions sealed the deal for espresso. One was the invention of mechanized high pressure to make the espresso shot, or drink. Another was the development of steam wands to foam milk for cappuccinos, or espresso shots with milk added.

"Does any home espresso maker beat the serious Capresso?"

Espresso drinks are judged differently by connoisseurs. Flavor components as acidity and various specific flavors from the individual bean are what we look for in regular brewed coffee; espresso is a much more created product. Much value is placed on the creation of a specific flavor profile and the preparation aspects. Espresso is tasted for flavor, but also for crema, a foam and physical characteristic of pressurized brewing.

Espresso offers obvious advantages to a coffee drinker who's searching for a wonderful fresh tasting coffee beverage away from home. Gone is the concern that you will arrive in a shop at the wrong time, namely an hour or so after a fresh batch of drip coffee is made. Your espresso is made "espressly" for you. To those in the espresso business the task is more complicated. Espresso requires very tight tolerances, in equipment and in preparation. Espresso grind is very picky. A little too coarse and the coffee will be weak and have no crema. If it's too fine, the machine can simply stop working. It's not unusual to see an experienced barista (Italian for the someone who's mastered making espresso) taking twenty or thirty minutes to set the grind before the first customer shot is made.

There are lots of variations on the shots. Here are the top and ones most likely to be on a menu in any café:

Espresso – any coffee drink made under pressure, referred to as a shot. Classic shot portion is one ounce. Less is called a short.

More is called, yep, a long. Espresso is typically made from beans in a blend and somewhat darker roasted. Blends are used because espresso's goal is to create a flavor rather than recreate the essence of one bean. Dark roasting is used because the high pressure spotlights acidity. Darker roasting subdues acidity in a complimentary way to espresso's spotlight.

Cappuccino – any drink made with foamed milk and espresso shot. The espresso shot is usually added after the milk is poured into a cup. In Italy the cappuccino is served in a six-ounce cup. In the U.S., the portion is larger. Consequently, many drinkers request two shots to maintain coffee flavor. Cappuccinos in Italy are likely to be served dry, or with much froth virtually sitting on top of the coffee shot. In the U.S., a more popular drink has at least some liquid milk in the coffee.

Americano – an espresso shot that is cut with hot water to offer a rough equivalent in volume and strength to an American cup of drip coffee. Invented during World War II for visiting U.S. soldiers but has had lasting value.

Latté – any drink that has both steamed and foamed milk in it. It differs from a cappuccino mostly in the amount of milk. Be careful, in Italy ordering a latté may result in plain cold milk. Latté is milk in Italian. The correct name is café latté. Trivia: The café latte is the most popular of all espresso coffee drinks served in America.

Machiatto – an espresso drink with a slight amount of foamed milk added. In some ways a real sleeper drink and quite possibly the best way to discover the uniqueness of espresso without having to forgo milk.

Flavored drinks – flavors can be added to any coffee drink, but without a doubt the most popular place to use flavors is in espresso beverages. Many connoisseurs take an attitude against flavors, as if coffee is some kind of club and if you use flavors you don't belong. AN OPINION: Flavors are fine. After all, even among connoisseurs milk and sweeteners have been used throughout coffee history. Black coffee has a negative association throughout the world as a cowboy and police-only drink to stay awake. Yet as fun as flavors can be, many people have never really had the chance to sample the flavor of coffee by itself. Meanwhile, most espresso drinks allow the drinker to add flavors using syrups, a preferred method because flavors added to beans can become impossible to remove from machines.

Breve – any espresso drink done short in time and size. The breve is sort of a concentrated espresso. It's fun to try but probably not different enough for most coffee drinkers.

ESPRESSO: IS IT A FAD OR A TREND?

I still get asked this question all the time: "Is the craze for espresso drinks in this country a fad or a trend?" At this point the interviewer cites the hula hoop, Silly Putty, or, if they're old enough or historically-minded, speak-easies of the 1920s. I've been asked a variant of this question so often, the answer is beginning to sound over-rehearsed: "The 'craze' for a certain style coffee house is more akin to the fashion industry than to specialty coffee. In this way I'd expect to hire a new decorator for a coffee shop every two years. Ditto the "coffee jargon" that is considered "hip" in certain cities in the Northwest. To many in the East and Midwest, it sounds overly cute and even provincial.

"However, as for espresso as a coffee preparation method, it is here to stay. There are too many good reasons for its acceptance in the marketplace, reasons I don't see going away." Too long for a sound bite, perhaps, but it is my honest answer.

Consider this. You and your significant other walk into a restaurant (or a coffee bar, for that matter) and want to order a perfect cup. You note the menu offers both filter coffee and espresso. What to you do?

If you're like me, you try to crane your neck to find the coffee-brewing island and then make a visual analysis of whether the coffee might be fresh. Is there a grinder? Does it seem as if anyone has cleaned the pot and remade the coffee during the past twenty minutes? Are they using enough coffee to differentiate the brew from tea?

Should the answer to any of these questions be "No," then you might well wish to order espresso. Why? I thought you'd never ask.

Espresso will probably be made fresh. There's very little advantage in making espressos in advance of your request, although I confess I've seen it done. Second, most restaurateurs know too little about espresso to try to cheat by using less coffee than is optimum.

They are intimidated by the seeming complexity of the machine. So far, most do what they are told. And espresso machines, they are told, won't brew properly if the proper amount of grounds aren't shoveled into it. And ground according to brewer instructions. As if freshness, proper measurements and grind weren't reasons enough, many restaurants that continue to poison patrons with non-dairy coffee "whiteners" that contain cheaper to buy-and-store, hydrogenated fats rather than milk products, are happy to provide low-fat milk for their cappuccinos and lattés.

The real drinks of course, are not espressos at all, but rather the lattés and cappuccinos. If you are curious, do what I did. I sat one morning at a Starbucks and counted the drinks served. Two espressos the entire morning. Mine was one (I had to order something to reduce their suspicions.)

Here's a question that I don't get asked too often but is really more interesting: "Is all coffee moving towards espresso?"

Here the answer gets trickier. Hmm. Well... No, the answer is "no".

Here's why: First, reason number one for espresso catching on in restaurants is a matter of convenience for them and trust for you. The restaurant makes more profit because it throws away less product, unless they are foolish enough to make drinks that aren't ordered.

This reason doesn't exist at home. After all, you can better predict when you want your coffee and make the right amount. You can also certainly trust yourself to know you made it fresh.

After reading this book, you should already be a believer in using the proper grind and measurements.

So, in non-food service applications at least, some of the allure of espresso goes away.

Or does it? As lovers of coffee, we must not rule out the most important reason for our attraction to the bean—the taste. Espresso is a relevant and distinguished method for extraction. While I stop short of calling it the best method (that's like the best chord on a piano) I would say it offers a taste and flavor all its own. In this regard I wish to proclaim espresso as a welcome additional preparation method for Americans. Anyone who believes consumers won't either spend the extra amount for an espresso maker or accept one of the low-cost almost-espresso makers has their eyes closed.

The challenge, in this case, is not to create a market, which appears to exist already, but to find an affordable way to satisfy it. The technology needed to create water pressure used to extract a perfect espresso beverage is NASA-level, compared to the easy going filter-drip machines we are used to buying. And, as any software buyer knows, technology has its price.

Therefore, I will be following the developments high and low, for the ultimate brewer in addition to our beloved filter makers.

Either way, it's all coffee to me. And I like it.

Coffee Gallery

Chapter Ten

Coffee, Food and Recipes

Coffee Inspiration

"Remember, how short my time is." Psalm 89:47

There's a bumper sticker that says, "Life's too short to drink bad coffee". Hardly original, but fits right in with the more profound Psalm quoted above. The truth is, life's too short to do anything with carelessness. Our friends and family, our relationship with God, all outrank any simple secular pleasure. Yet, I find that often the sensate pleasure of something as simple as a great cup of coffee with a friend offers much in transmitting my own fondness of that friendship to them. I know how pleased I am when I have coffee at a friend's and they tell me they want to brew it just right knowing how much I appreciate it. It sure starts the visit off right.

10

COFFEE, FOOD AND RECIPES

It's nothing for a wine connoisseur to spend a long time reading the wine list before getting just the right bottle to share over dinner. Why doesn't the coffee connoisseur? I'll tell you why. Practical brewing limitations make it difficult to offer multiple types of coffee for different foods. In a perfect world they would.

In certain situations coffee's mix with food is very carefully considered. A great pancake house will test many different coffees before finding one that will taste best with its signature pancakes.

The obvious industry nod to coffee's blending with food is after-dinner coffee. For years, after-dinner coffee has been roasted darker, a fuller-bodied blend and even brewed stronger, all with the purpose of standing the coffee right up next to a highly-flavored dinner bill of face.

Here is my guide to coffee mixing with food. As with every recommendation in this book, don't let it challenge any views of your own. Everyone's own taste buds and saliva are different enough that the rules can't be hard and fast, just as with any food or beverage recommendations.

Breakfast – Breakfast foods generally work best with more "acidy" coffees. One reason South American and African coffees are so popular for breakfast is their high acidity. The bright high notes in such coffees are gentle wake-up calls to your senses, and smell great as well. A Colombian, Kenya or perhaps Hawaiian Kona. Superior Coffee's Kona blend is all three, and I know a restaurateur who absolutely stands by the combination. His business is mostly breakfast. I also testify to the lighter roasted coffees. Even so-called low acidity coffees like

Sumatras can be downright acidy when they're lighter roasted. Remember, when I say acidy I don't mean harsh, I mean bright.

Generally, the lighter roasted, acidy coffees do best with the typical American breakfast foods. Kenya, Hawaii, Brazil, Costa Rica, Guatemala. These are the classics that blend best with pastries, pancakes, breakfast meats and whole grains.

The dinner foods make it more complicated. While breakfast nooks couldn't dream of surviving without the very finest and carefully chosen blend or variety and roast, even so-called white tablecloth restaurants often serve coffee that either clashes or is just lacklustre compared to their food. I believe this is because they haven't realized that it makes a difference. Oddly, they simply buy the same coffee the breakfast places use. Too bad, it makes quite a difference.

When you think dinner, think body. I find that Sumatra is a coffee that goes with almost any food. Like a robust wine, it can stand up to almost any taste. And, it's not really a question of body. The myth is that body is increased by darker (longer) roasting. Not true. Dark roasting highlights certain flavors and increases a carmelization factor. But, body can actually appear to reduce as roasting times increase.

Heavier foods like salmon with teriyaki marinade, roast of beef and lamb dishes beg for hearty, robust coffees. Even lighter foods will work better with heavier coffees. Gravies and sauces add an additional flavor burden that must be matched by a strong coffee.

BEST COMBINATIONS

Pastries, pancakes, cereals: Colombia, Mexican
Chicken: Guatemalan, Costa Rican
White fish: Mexican
Salmon: Yemen Mocha
Beef Stew, Lamb Chops: Sumatran, Tanzanian

My last note on this is, again, don't regard these as rules. Your own palate and the spices and flavorings you use will influence the decision of which coffees best accompany your food. My point is to start considering the combination, whatever it is.

What to do when you have the wrong coffee: If you have an overbearing coffee with a milder food, what do you do? Brew it more weakly. My method is to brew the same, but to dilute the coffee with an additional portion of hot water. If the food is strong but the coffee is light, just do the reverse. Use more ground coffee. In the days when restaurants prided themselves on fine after-dinner coffees, it was customary to add an extra scoop to a dinner coffee. It makes just as much sense today. Be the one in your community to discover it first. You'll be surprised at how many people will ask for more, or simply ask for coffee at all, if your other guests have smacked their lips after trying your better matched coffee.

Coffee Recipes

How do I do this and still remain a Christian? I feel about recipes that same way I do about tea: I don't like to use up my maximum caffeine intake on anything but real, true blue, fresh brewed coffee. That said, I know some people won't buy any book unless it has some killer recipes in it. The good news is that there are some wonderful coffee/food combinations.

Shea Sturdivant, a wonderful Southern belle (and college professor) who is one of my best coffee drinking buddies, put her own book out years ago. In it she gave some wonderful recipes that feature her bold Southern-style taste. Meanwhile, here are some others that I've seen and tried over the years that you will find savory. My recommendation is still: eat small portions, so you can still drink a cup of perfect coffee afterwards.

My own quest to discover healthy foods (I'm actually convinced the term is an oxymoron) has prompted me to collect recipes that utilize other foods that have a reputation for being healthy. Trust, however, that I've rejected any recipe that doesn't taste good to my palate. I wouldn't include something just to meet political correctness standards.

Recipes

Coffee Walnuts

    3 cups walnut halves
    1 cup brown sugar
    1/2 cup white sugar
    1/2 cup sour cream
    1 tablespoon coffee concentrate
    1 teaspoon vanilla
    1/2 teaspoon ginger (optional)

Combine all the ingredients except the vanilla, coffee and optional ginger in a sauce pan. Stir until it becomes a solid. Take it off the burner and stir in the vanilla and ginger. Add the walnuts, making sure each one is nicely coated. Put the walnuts on a buttered baking sheet. I like to keep a few of these in the refrigerator. My kids like to freeze them...so far no broken teeth.

    A company called Victoria House makes a decent coffee concentrate. There's an even better one made by some Trappist monks available from Armeno Coffee Roasters in Northborough, Mass.

Coffee Cake Icing

Everyone wants a coffee icing for a birthday cake.

    1 2/3 cups confectioners' sugar
    1/2 cup butter
    1/4 teaspoon salt
    3 tablespoons coffee concentrate
    1 teaspoon vanilla

The usual "beat the butter" till it's soft. Then start adding the sugar, slowly so it mixes up evenly. Add the salt and coffee. Once the mixture starts to cool off, add the vanilla. After letting it stand for around five minutes, start beating it again to whip it up. You're ready to spread it on your layer cake.

Coffee Salad Dressing

I got this one from a marketing piece prepared by the Kona coffee people, who always seem anxious to throw money at any subject as long as they can keep Kona coffee prominently displayed. And, in fact, I have made this dressing with various coffees, distilled into concentrates and I think Kona is the best. I believe one Mary Van Camp is the author of the original recipe.

1 Tablespoon shallots, minced
1 cup coffee vinegar (cook 1 cup coffee beans in 2 cups champagne vinegar until reduced and infused.)
3 Tablespoons chopped coffee beans (*see note below)

1 Tablespoon minced garlic

2 egg yolks

2 Tablespoons honey

1/2 Tablespoon salt

5 cups salad oil (I prefer soy)

Whisk together shallots, garlic and vinegar. Add yolks with honey and salt. Emulsify by slowly whisking in salad oil. The original author suggest throwing some instant Kona coffee granules as a final step. Since I don't believe in instant coffee on principle, I'd just say you should do it if you want. I actually take a few Kona coffee beans and grind them up and toss 'em in. I imagine (probably the right word) that it tastes better.

Coffee Gingerbread

This one also appears in the Kona book, credited to Michelle Ono, but I originally got it from someone else. Forgive me if it's yours. I have a distinct fondness for all things ginger, especially when they include my other favorite spice, cloves.

1 cup brewed Kona coffee

2 teaspoons baking soda (non-alum type is better, I use Rumsford - that oughta be worth a case of the stuff)

1 teaspoon powdered ginger

1 teaspoon chopped fresh ginger (for an extra kick – this is my addition)

1/4 teaspoon ground cloves

1/2 cup sugar

1/2 cup molasses (I use unsulfured)

2 cups sifted flour

1 teaspoon cinnamon

1/2 teaspoon nutmeg

1/2 cup butter

1/2 cup brown sugar

2 eggs

Butter a 9 by 12" baking pan. Dust the pan with flour. Preheat your oven to 350 degrees F. Sift together flour, baking soda, powdered ginger, cinnamon, nutmeg and cloves. In a bowl, beat the butter, sugar and eggs, adding molasses once the others have cooperated. Beat until it's creamy and thick. Stir in "room temperature "coffee. Add flour mixture. Stir. Then pour the batter into a pan. Bake for 45 minutes, until the sides start withdrawing a little from the pan, which means it's done. Leave it in the pan while it cools.

Coffee Ice Cream

This is one recipe that my mother added. She'll probably sue me because she wants to publish her own book, right after publishing her "Sonny Dearest" expose of me. To be fair, I'm going to resist publishing her peach ice cream recipe, which is even better. Okay, Mom, I'm going to risk it.

- *4 eggs*
- *2 1/2 cups sugar*
- *7 cups milk*
- *3 cups whipping cream (yes, the same stuff doctors tell you not to use)*
- *1 1/2 teaspoons vanilla*
- *1 1/2 tablespoons coffee concentrate*
- *1/2 teaspoon salt*

Beat eggs until light. Add the sugar... slowly. Beat until it thickens. Add everything else and mix for... eternity. Freeze, preferably in a standard 5 quart ice cream container.

Paul Kalenian, of Armeno Coffee in Northborough, Mass., once taste tested two coffees, one made with Sumatra and one made with Colombian coffees. The Sumatra out-tasted the Colombian by far. My point is that different coffees significantly change the flavor. I'd recommend the Trappist coffee syrup, or a Honduran coffee concentrate called Purjava from the company, Tenback.

Coffee Fudge

I've obviously gotten of my pompous high-horse nonsense about health foods, haven't I? I think you practically have to put a Surgeon General's warning on this one. But, it's delicious.

- 2 cups sugar
- 1 cup coffee
- 1 tablespoon butter
- 1/4 teaspoon salt
- 1/4 teaspoon cream of tartar
- 1/2 teaspoon almond extract
- 1 cup pecan pieces

Stir the coffee, butter, cream of tartar and salt together over a low heat until all the sugar turns liquid; turn up the heat and bring to a quick boil. It should become a kind of soft ball that you can imagine would almost hold its shape if you formed it. Once this happens, remove the heat and let it cool just a bit.

Now, add the almond extract and beat until it begins to harden. Then, add the pecans and pour it (shovel is more like it) onto a buttered cookie sheet. You know the rest.

Special Coffee Beverages

I consider these recipes because they are not straight brewed coffee. Some coffee connoisseurs consider flavored coffees to be beneath their hallowed palates. Come on! If you put cream and sugar in your coffee you're drinking flavored coffee. There's no credibility to the argument against flavored coffee. I once had a custom blended coffee with an apricot flavor added. It was absolutely wonderful. A common myth spread by snobbish roasters is that flavored coffees are a way their competitors use up lacklustre

beans. The truth is, like any blend, the parts are very critical to the blend.
Here are a few coffee recipes for other than straight coffee you might enjoy:

Clove coffee

I like this one. Cloves are very good for you. They help clean your system of parasites. Cloves are a secret ingredient in many other beverages. I often sprinkle ground cloves into coffee, especially around Christmas. But in the summer, iced coffee tastes great with cloves. I have a friend who went further. She puts the non-ground whole cloves into her brew basket. I normally don't recommend putting flavors into brewers because they forever add some taste. But since she uses the Chemex, which is glass, it simply washes away. If she doesn't add cloves next time, there will be no taste.

By the way, cloves are great in tea.

> **Brew one pot of coffee**
> **Add one shake of ground cloves**

Iced coffee

Iced coffee is a great way to refresh yourself in the summer. Even in my native Illinois climate, summers are hot. I usually drink iced coffee in the afternoon, whenever the temperature is over 85 degrees F.

> **1 pot freshly brewed coffee**
> **Ice cubes made from that coffee**
> **Cream and sweeten to taste**

Iced coffee is actually the most critical coffee to make, because at cooler temperatures any bitterness will be instantly apparent. The biggest mistake most people make is leaving their morning coffee on a burner all morning and then trying

to resuscitate it over ice later that day. If you want the best iced coffee, switch off your coffee maker the moment the coffee is done brewing. Another brilliant idea I must have heard from someone else (but I'll take the credit) is to make a tray of ice cubes from coffee. That way, as you sip your afternoon coffee you will find it stays nice and strong as you drink it. The melting ice cubes will simply be more great coffee. The fanatics among us (my own hand is raised) will wish to experiment with making ice cubes from different coffees from the one being drunk.

Dessert Island Coffees

In the event of a tragedy such as my plane becoming lost in the Pacific, I would hope that, short of rescue, I would be blessed with the following short list of provisions:

Dessert Island emergency coffee making kit

- *1 mini-pint Chemex, with a ten-year supply of half-moon shaped filters*
- *1 Zassenhaus manual hand grinder, which just so happens to grind exactly enough coffee in its chamber to fill the Chemex coffee maker.*
- *1 approved coffee measure*
- *Ten year supply of Volvic bottled spring water, or Pur water pitcher*

Dessert Island coffee beans

La Minita Costa Rican

Yemen Mocha

Sumatra Mandheling

Ethiopian Sidamo

Aged Java

My own special blend, which includes aged Colombian, Ethiopian Sidamo and Sumatran

I sometimes sit back and imagine sitting there on my island enjoying a wonderful cup of coffee while watching the waves roll in and a beautiful orange sunset as a backdrop.

Coffee Gallery

Chapter Eleven

COFFEE, CAFFEINE AND HEALTH

Pan-American Coffee Bureau circa 1953

Just what the Doctor ordered

Coffee Inspiration

Jesus: "It is not the healthy who need a doctor, but the sick. I have not come to call the righteous, but sinners to repentance." Luke 5:5

The analogy to coffee here is so obvious, but writers are paid by words, not simply pointing out the obvious. If there was just good coffee being served in the world, there would be no reason for this book. There is a trend to refer to any habit as an addiction. The only thing that makes me believe that coffee is addictive is seeing someone drink bad coffee... and finish the cup. I don't drink bad coffee. I wait until I find a cup that satisfies. I do however drink less-than-tasty coffee in social situations, or in situations where I might embarrass someone who's trying to please me. There, the warmth of the cup, the shared ritual is enough to overcome the physical defects.

But, there is much bad coffee served. Coffee is a product that is fragile and requires expertise to prepare it. Rather than refer to readers as sinners in search of repentance, I prefer to view us all as seekers who aspire to a better world. A major truth in the world of coffee is, once you've had a truly wonderful and taste-satisfying cup of coffee, you are destined to want another – and to share one with a friend. In this way, coffee is directly akin to Christianity.

11

Coffee, Caffeine and Health

Wow! Maybe it's just the Starbucks' stock, but the medical profession, which is like the Midwest weather, can always be counted on to change its mind, has been weighing in on coffee. Deepak Chopra, who is far enough removed from Christianity to pass the secular humanist litmus test, has come out giving coffee a nice plug. Chopra even goes as far as to suggest that coffee drinkers live longer.

The more recent *Live Right For Your Type*, a creative if not definitive take on the whole "blood types as diet indicators" theory, says great things about coffee... if you are the right type that is. Dr Peter J. D'Amato's view is that Type As and Bs actually benefit from coffee's acidity in aiding digestion. Good news for Type A, me. But, if you're Type O, he suggests tea instead. Ouch.

My own opinion, as I said on *Oprah* and elsewhere, is that coffee has been with us for over a thousand years and, it would seem that coffee drinkers and non-coffee drinkers live to just about the same old age.

I've spent enough time researching old articles from two hundred years ago until now. The medical community is consistent only in its ability to switch sides every few years.

WHY COFFEE IS SUCH A HEALTH ITEM, PRO OR CON

If coffee has such a non-controversial bill of health, why the constant controversy? Are government agencies so fund heavy or researchers so eager? Obviously, this is a larger question than this book is designed to answer. But, actually, coffee got some help along the way largely thanks to some yellow journalism in the seventeenth century.

My friend and colleague, Ian Bersten, has written about it extensively in his scholarly *Coffee, Sex and Health* book (Helian Books) and I'm going to give you the Cliffs Notes version here.

Basically, if you've seen any old coffee reproductions, you've likely seen one called the Maiden's Complaint Against Coffee. You might assume from the title that this was some kind of political movement started up by seventeenth century women. It may interest you to know that the author was a man, and one with some conflict of interest as well. Just as coffeehouses currently have stolen business away from the local bars, so it was in the 1600s. Men who previously frequented taverns switched to coffeehouses. My friend Bersten's pet theory is that this pamphlet was written and distributed by a tavern owner as a kind of negative spin. Reading it, one is aware of the author's implications that coffee is a depressant. I know the cover has been reproduced often, but as far as I know, it is seldom read. It should be. Like the 1960s Warren Report, the Maiden's Complaint Against Coffee is its own worst enemy.

I will present just a sample of the kind of authoritative evidence that is presented:

One of the characters is named Snapshort. Snapshort is agreeing with the supposed protagonists and offers this to say about his caffeine experience:

"I went into a coffeehouse and took a dish of that hell-burnt liquor, thinking to settle my brains in their right center. With the rattling noises of kettles, skimmers and ladles (early espresso equipment no doubt) among the braziers, my brains run round as swift as a windmill, and all my joints are as dead as an old woman's troubled with the dead palsy. I then went to Moorfields (a tavern) and took a turn in the usurer's walk, where I drank a cup of good, wholesome ale, with which I was revived, enlivened and restored to my memory so perfectly, that I had an account in my head of every penny due to my master since creation."

Pretty compelling evidence, isn't it? Of course, there was an answer "document" that was equally silly, which claimed that the women of England "live on an island of paradise." So my view stands. Coffee is neither very good or very bad.

THE STORY ON CAFFEINE

When once asked by an audience member if caffeine was something to be concerned about, a doctor said, "I wouldn't lose any sleep over it". So sums up much of the research that has been done over the past hundred years

Caffeine has a profound effect upon the nervous system. It can keep you alert and boost the mood and even the immune system in some individuals. Others seem to be virtually free from any effects.

Coffee, of course, contains caffeine. So do teas, both black and green. So does chocolate. Naturally, coffee is the focus here. Let's dispel some myths:

Since Decafs claim to be 97% caffeine free, coffee must be 100% caffeine.

Espresso is the most high-octane coffee drink.

Dark roast coffees are virtually caffeine-free.

All specialty coffees are higher in caffeine.

Brewing coffee full strength increases the caffeine.

DECAF – 97% CAFFEINE-FREE VS. COFFEE 100% CAFFEINE

Decaffeinated coffee is 97% caffeine-free. That means that 97% of the caffeine has been removed. Actually, the amount of caffeine removed is closer to a theoretical 100%, but the original Sanka

advertising agency suggested 97% as "catchier" sounding. All coffee is chemically 97% caffeine free. Caffeine is less than 1% of even the strongest cup of coffee. In decaf, 97% of the less-than 1% is removed.

ESPRESSO = HIGH CAFFEINE/HIGH OCTANE COFFEE

Espresso is actually, ounce per ounce, lower in caffeine than regular coffee. The reason? Espresso is brewed under pressure very quickly, less than thirty seconds. Caffeine, regardless of its reputation for "speed" comes forth rather slowly during brewing. Much of the caffeine is never given time to extract in espresso. While espresso is hardly decaf, it is relatively low in caffeine compared to a cup of regular coffee. The fact that so many people claim otherwise probably has to do with psychological effects reinforced by espresso's flavor punch.

DARK ROAST – VIRTUAL DECAF?

Dark roast coffees are sometimes claimed to be lower in caffeine. This is true in that caffeine is slowly burned off during roasting and dark roast coffees are roasted longer. Of course bean weight per volume also goes down during roasting. If coffee is weighed for brewing, a common and recommended commercial practice, the caffeine content difference becomes arguable and ultimately... negligible.

SPECIALTY COFFEES – POWERFUL FLAVOR MEANS MORE CAFFEINE

Specialty coffees actually come from a lower caffeine source. There are two commercially available coffee types: Arabica and Robusta. Virtually all specialty coffee except for some specific espresso blends are arabica. Robusta is used predominantly in blends found in cheap canned coffees. Arabica coffees generally contain about half the caffeine of robustas. Just to be fair, arabica coffees do not contain a more pungent flavor, in fact the big promoted advertising advantage used to promote robusta in the 1950s was its ability to produce coffee flavor using less measured coffee. The flavor of arabicas is milder, and subjectively more pleasant. While some robustas are good coffees, it is probably fair to say that all the world's great coffees are arabica.

BREWING FULL STRENGTH – CAFFEINE WALLOP!

This myth is unconsciously spread every time someone says, "Oh, use less coffee when you make it, I don't like it strong!" If too little coffee is used, those grounds will be overtaxed making the coffee taste very strong and very harsh. It makes no difference how much caffeine will be extracted. The best way to reduce the harsh bitterness in most people's coffee is to grind coarser, which will speed up the extraction process in automatic drip machines, reducing bitterness and caffeine. It will still be caffeinated coffee, however. The only way to get decaffeinated coffee is to use coffees treated to remove their caffeine.

DECAF

Decaffeinated coffee is coffee that has had the caffeine removed. Currently, there are two methods in common use. One uses a chemical solvent. The solvent most commonly used is methyline chloride. Its adherents, including of course its marketing firms but also experts, claim taste advantages, an important factor since all decaffeination processes remove at least some precious coffee flavor. The second popular method is water process, commonly called "Swiss Water" after the firm that originated it. Swiss Water advocates claim it is inherently inert, with no possible health effects or environmental impact.

Most coffee experts are able to tell a decaf coffee because of flavor losses in the process. Roasters almost routinely roast decafs darker to attempt to boost the perceived flavor. However, some people have no choice but to drink decaf. You should probably try several to discover one that meets your own taste standards.

DECAF'S FUTURE

Decaffeinated coffee has always been done after the fact. There are projects underway to remove the caffeine botanically. That's right, a decaffeinated coffee tree. Obviously, if a peach can be grown without fur (the nectarine) then a decaf coffee tree seems likely. Since a lot of the coffee drunk by high-end connoisseurs is consumed exclusively for taste, it seems like a good idea.

Coffee Gallery

Chapter Twelve

POLITICS AND BEAN COUNTS

Fresh roasted

Coffee Inspiration

"For you have need of patience, that after you have done the will of God, you [mig]ht receive the promise." Hebrews 10:36

[M]ost people do not make coffee properly. Part of the reason is that, unlike [mos]t other beverages, coffee has never been successfully prepackaged. The [indu]stry has failed to teach, due to politics and in-fighting. My goal in writing this [boo]k is to take offer some real-world ways of empowering anyone who reads and [is wi]lling to try something new. I'm no scholar, but I've been patient. Along the [way,] I've made a lot of bad coffee. I've read most of what's been written before. I [admi]re a lot of the writing, but the authors were, for the most part, not as willing [to wo]rk from scratch. Learning to make great coffee is hardly finding a cure for [disea]se, but I have learned to learn and I try to take that approach to everything [else.] I can't wait for the first time I run into someone who's motivated by this [book] to try their own experiments and makes me a great cup of coffee. My success [will] be your success.

12

Politics and Recounts

Politics and coffee have a long history together. Coffee is the world's oldest smart drug that stimulates both thinking and conversation. As I write this the recent U.S. presidential election has sparked me to see the whole concept of bean counting a different way. I'm sure glad that coffee growers don't use the current election system we use to count votes to count beans.

In the first place, we'd never have coffee. The coffee beans would be constantly be recounted; while consumers would sit empty-cupped in agony. At least say this for our politicians – no one misses either that much. I suppose the upside of coffee recounts is the delays would restore to the market the aged coffee, unroasted beans that mellow by being in storage. History has yet to record whether our two presidential candidates will so mellow.

Second, the risk exists that the beans would not be recounted at all. The margin for error would rise. Maybe this or that bean would no longer qualify and be thrown away. Or even more humiliating... be sold as tea.

A third possibility is that coffee growers would be asked to reexamine the beans to see if they were really what they appeared to be. Picking up a handful, the examiner might decide that these beans did not intend to be, say, Colombian Supremo after all. Feeling a little more, she might well project that the beans intended all along to be Yemen Mocha. This scenario has actually been tried, when for years a certain Hawaiian exporter had fine but underpriced Costa Rican coffee beans shipped to him in Hawaii, where he relabeled them 100% Kona. To think he was convicted of a crime and he didn't do much except touch the beans to force chubs to fall out on the floor.

Bean counting is at least a revered and respected profession. I mean, it's a common term, "Bean counter". Vote counting? It doesn't come close. Vote stealing is a more common term, and likely a more common practice. I am just old enough to recall the 1960 presidential campaign. Who in Chicago (where I grew up) could forget how our esteemed Mayor Richard Daley mysteriously "found" just enough votes to place John Kennedy in the White House?

The current players just don't come close to the style and panache of the old time politicians, who were at least entertaining in their ruthlessness. Just as bankers lack the personality of street hoodlums, the new generation of politicians are all too dry and lackluster. Coffee doesn't appear to run that risk at least.

Maybe that's why consumers like coffee more than politicians. I know it's true for me.

Coffee Gallery

Chapter Thirteen

COFFEE MYTHS

Pan-American Coffee
Bureau circa 1953

Mmm, Coffee... Mom knows what hits the spot!

Coffee Inspiration

Jesus: "I will open my mouth in parables, I will utter things hidden since the creation of the world." Matthew 13:24

I've always found the Bible to be a creative book. I mean, what's more creative than building a kingdom of God? What's more creative than imagining a world based on forgiveness? Of everlasting life? If there's one method of education creative people respond to, it's analogies. Parables are analogies set to stories.

While I can't promise to deliver a book as creative as the Bible, I can guarantee that you'll brew the best coffee from this book. I still recommend the Bible for its vast "other" resources. By the way, there's a well-known and well-marketed herb tea product that recommends in its ingredients "the chants of a shaman," or something similar. I do recommend adding a prayer to the coffee making ritual. I truly to like thank the Lord for all my earthly joys. Fine coffee is among them.

13

Coffee Myths

Fibs of the Business, the Culture, the Customer

An important part of the coffee culture is the endless stream of bunk-derived opinions, fibs, half-truths and downright lies concerning every aspect of growing, choosing and brewing our favorite beverage. To be fair (and I don't really know why this concerns me) many in the trade are not dishonest but idealistic and have themselves been the victims of age-old misconceptions about their products.

Much of coffee is so subjective. The product itself, being of nature, is unreliable in a beautiful way. This means a green broker may get excited about a bean that never again tastes the same way. Is it the odd crop? Did the green broker have different tastebuds that day? It's all so vague.

Coffee is just like sociology. We all agree that generalizations are practically worthless, but without them we can no longer study our subject.

Make sense?

The fascinating aspect of coffee is that we can sit around discussing something that we can not really fully touch with mere words. At any rate, here we go on our journey into the real world of jive, the great lies of coffee.

Inside the Business (Or what your roaster must put up with)

1 It's Blue Mountain

2 It's better than Blue Mountain

3 You can blend it with Blue Mountain and that'll be better than just Blue Mountain straight

4 The label is wrong. It's Blue Mountain, but I got a great deal on some mislabeled bags.

5 You can substitute Peruvian. None of your customers can tell the difference and you'll save $.10 per pound.

Inside the Specialty Store (Or what your roaster may tell you)

1) It's Blue Mountain.

2) Real Blue Mountain is no longer any good. Kona has richer soil.

3) I roast it dark to bring out all the flavor. Anyone who roasts lighter is just trying to sell you weight (bonus points - two lies in one statement).

4) We buy richer beans so you can use less coffee per pot.

5) We roast everything in _____ (any city will do, extra points for Seattle). But nothing is ever sold more than two weeks following roasting. Sometimes the beans are still warm when they come off the delivery truck.

6) You can grind an arabica bean finer and use less coffee per pot.

7) The reason Hawaiian is better is they genetically spliced the coffee plant with the marijuana plant in the early 1970s when two rock stars bought the plantation. There's much more than caffeine in Kona (roaster must flash knowing look towards customer's girlfriend). I ran into this lie only once, but I thought it was so wonderful, I couldn't resist.

Coffee Myths

Lies grocery stores tell everybody:

1) With our freshness bags, the coffee stays fresh forever.

2) Our high-yield blend lets you use less, so you save more.

3) We offer 100% Blue Mountain coffee, too. So there's no reason to go to a specialty store.

4) The reason the Hills Brothers can sell their coffee for less is they buy a whole country's crop at once. Then they pass along the savings to you. It's kind of like a buying club.

5) Some guy with an oversized sample roaster can't possibly roast coffee as accurately as our giant quality-assured plant in Cincinnati. Did you know that our roasting units were designed by the same people who built the space shuttle? 6) Coffee is coffee. It all travels on the same ship. The truth is, no one knows where any particular bean comes from, once it's roasted.

7) Nestles did a secret research paper seven years ago that proves that the six biggest chefs in the restaurant business couldn't tell the difference between top-grade Costa Rican coffee and freeze-dried instant Taster's Choice. And when they could taste a difference, they invariably went for the Taster's Choice.

Lies coffee maker manufacturers tell:

1) You can use less with our high-ex method and still enjoy a robust cup.

2) We spent ten million dollars developing a new extraction method. Did you know our designer worked for Proctor and Gamble and before that, helped build the space shuttle?

3) Ten grams per cup? Hey, you load up one of our coffee makers with that much coffee and you're practically drinking espresso. Here, the formulas right here on the can of coffee I used this morning. One level teaspoon per cup. But, make it how you like. It's your money.

4) Okay, I agree with you. Our $99 cappuccino maker is no match for a commercial unit. But we serve our customers and they asked

for it in a big way. There's no way you can make a real espresso for $99 and you and I know it. (Actually, the lie here isn't spoken. The lie, as I see it, is calling something an espresso maker that doesn't really make espresso. Kind of like a personal ad where someone says they're thirty and a stock broker when they're really sixty and a broke stocker (at Wal-Mart). Personally, I think one is no better than the other. It's a question of honesty.

The One Big Lie the Consumer Tells the Specialty Store

Wow, $10 per pound! I don't think I can afford to drink coffee at that price. It's cheaper to drink champagne. (note: At $30 per pound, coffee becomes in-line, price-wise, with average wine.)

The Drink That Refused to Go Away

Coffee almost died in the marketplace of the 1970s. What was once an honorable, pleasurable drink was almost run out of town by bad beans, bad brewing and overzealous doctors. The coffee renaissance began with the emergence of the small batch roaster. Like all great eras, it can be traced to a small group of people, some working together, most not.

ROASTING REVOLUTION

For instance, Michael Sivetz, a General Foods employee who worked in South America developing (of all things) giant instant coffee plants, is one of the heroes. Michael built the first small batch roasters, or at least the first ones that anyone remembers. His invention was perfectly matched to the time and energy requirements of the time period. The large plants roasted (and still do) with large drums that revolve over a flame for twenty minutes. Sivetz' roasters were like oversize air corn poppers. The result was the ability to roast small batches of coffee right in a store.

GREAT GREEN COFFEE

Of course a roaster is meaningless without great raw, or green coffee to fill it up each day. Fortunately, the large commodity roasters were convinced that postwar GI's and their coffee making honeys were unmoved by such sissy moves like sipping their coffee and playing guessing games about where it came from. They were, after all, building a new great society and coffee was merely a human motor fuel. The major coffee companies' abandonment of great coffees meant these beans were cheap and plentiful to the early small-batch roasters. Erna Knutsen, a secretary for a large coffee broker, began to see opportunities with these beans her bosses passed over.

ESPRESSO

The Pacific Northwest is known for its independence. Juan Trippe, owner of Pan American Airlines, once said he speculated that Seattle must have something in the water that "kept people from listening to anyone else's ideas," due to his frustrations with Seattle-based Boeing. Seattle, Portland and even San Francisco each had developing espresso-based cultures around this same time, including their own cult of small-batch roasters to supply them. The Pacific Northwest had always had their own brand of coffee, mostly much darker roasted, dating back to the gold prospecting days, due to a misconception that dark roasting's shiny oil slick somehow "locked in" freshness. So, espresso was developing around this time, far away from New York and other Eastern cities that like to lay claim to any successful trends.

BREWING: THE MISSING LINK

During this emerging renaissance, the brewer remained stagnant. At first this appears a mystery. New photographic films

bring new cameras, the Autobahn brought new cars, the compact disc brought new players, the last an irony since the format itself was promoted as "perfect sound forever" implying any machine would do.

So what went wrong with coffee?

THE TROUBLE WITH ENTREPRENEURS

Throughout history we find failed heroes. It's no different with coffee. The very same folks who reintroduced the great varieties of coffee beans we find today had one very large collective blind spot. They simply refuse to understand that great beans require great brewing. In this way, even the greatest coffee entrepreneurs are self-interested to a fault. Let me give you a great example. There is a pretty competent roaster named Kevin Knox. First of all, how could I dislike him: We're both Irish-Americans – he's even got my first name. He sends me free coffee, some of his best. And, I truly believe he's one of the best cuppers in the biz. His company, Allegro Coffee, has, with Caribou, done an outstanding job delivering a variety of coffees to the public on a large scale, proving it can be done.

Here's the rub: When a tiny operator like Larry Schlaeger pretty much lived on the edge trying to get his reproduced Flavor Seal Vacuum maker onto the market, I asked Kevin if he'd consider getting it into Whole Foods, where I thought it would do a great business. Kevin didn't lift a finger (in my view) to help. Why? I don't honestly know. In fact, Kevin goes out of his way to recommend the vacuum method on one of his coffee varieties. But, he doesn't help a guy who's mortgaged his house to produce one.

Sorry to pick on Kevin, who I still like even though he'll probably never talk to me again after this is published. Kevin Knox is not the only one. The coffee business is full of this kind of thinking.

Most of the marketing people fail to see the big picture. They work on their own cog all right. But, they still don't get it. Coffee isn't wine. Anyone with a ten dollar bill can become an alcoholic and enjoy some pretty fair taste experiences on the way. But, coffee requires that extra step. I would get anyone I can to deliver a better cup of coffee using average beans than they can using the finest.

By the way, whatever happened to Larry Schlaeger and the Flavor Seal? Last I heard, Larry had become disgusted with the coffee business and looked to other avenues to sell his product. Likewise, the Chemex, another great coffee maker, an American original that should be a standard. It's owner, the late Patrick Grassy, once told me that the people at coffee shows only care about their products. Why does the industry ignore coffee making?

EGO

There are a lot of reasons. One is shear entrepreneural ego. As a former standup comic, I remember appearing in improv groups with actors. One actor once told me about actors: "If you ain't talking about me, I ain't listening". Same with these small business men.

WINE FALLACY

I've already said it. Coffee may be like wine in that there are important taste differences. But, those differences are only important if it's brewed properly.

GREED

It's hard to get business people to get interested in coffee brewing equipment when the markup is so little. They're used to taking a few pennies' worth of coffee beans and selling cups of coffee for three dollars a cup. The truth is that the real money in coffee is made on liquid sales. The second poor relation is selling beans, where the money is at least doubled. When it comes to coffee makers, we're talking traditional home appliance markups, which are paltry at best.

COMPETITION

Mega retailers like Target or Wal-Mart sell coffee makers. It's pretty easy to see that only the most brilliant long-term strategist would see the wisdom of selling coffee gear.

THE GOOD GUYS, THE EXCEPTIONS

A brilliant, long-term strategist who does see the wisdom in this is Oren Bloostein, owner of Oren's Daily Roast in Manhattan. Oren knows he can't compete with large retailers. He sells coffee equipment anyway for all the right reasons. Mike Alburty, whose coffee business is a part of an Urbana, Illinois, health food store is another coffee visionary. Unfortunately, these exceptional individuals are few and far between in the coffee business.

So, brewing coffee remains a giant gap in how coffee is tasted. Honestly, I don't know how the coffee renaissance has grown as large as it has in this country, considering the average person still hasn't tasted truly great coffee. My guess is the smell of the beans is so overpowering that it has done most of the work. I'm also praying that this book, humbly written though it may be, will give consumers the empowerment they need to really give their precious beans life in the cup. For you. It's not smoking. It's not an elixir. It's coffee and that's good enough for me.

Coffee Gallery

Chapter Fourteen

RAINY DAY FEATURES

This slick Taster's Choice ad campaign distracted viewers away from lowly instant coffee

14

Coffee on Television

I wonder if we've considered the invaluable effect television characters had on our coffee drinking habits. No problem hitting the characters on the warm-hearted Andy of Mayberry was ever solved without Sheriff Andy Taylor making a trip to Aunt Bea's lace-curtained kitchen and pouring himself a cup from the percolator. My father had a somewhat different reaction to the trouble that boys make than television's Ward Cleaver. Ward should be brought back, if just to prove it is possible to have a cup of coffee to face every life challenge and still maintain calm. Although every episode I remember featured the electric percolator, there is a persistent rumor among coffee aficionados that there are early episodes showing a vintage vacuum coffee maker in June Cleaver's pristine kitchen.

Those impressed with the recent "Dream Team," must have forgotten Perry Mason. Raymond Burr, television's he-man lawyer who would have scoffed at the "power tie," took just fifty-four minutes each week to have his client found innocent rather than the sheepish not-guilty. Mason, fueled on coffee throughout the seemingly twenty-four hour days he worked, plowed through and did the police and prosecution's work as well, never ending a case until he produced the real murderer. No wonder the L.A. police have never recovered from his cancellation. Della Street, in Barbara Hale's superb and understated performance, insisted on bringing fresh coffee into every scene. I viewed one episode where Mason brought a half-dressed suspected damsel to Miss Street's apartment in order to hide the accused from Lieutenant Tragg. Three A.M. or not, Mason's secretary instinctively went to the kitchen and brought forth freshly brewed coffee.

Great Coffee

James Bond may have been the movies' first spy, but for most American kids, it took two spies, Napoleon Solo and Illya Kuriakan in The Man From UNCLE to really cement our relationship to these dogs of the Cold War. UNCLE headquarters was stocked with both young studs whose muscles were held in check by firearms in shoulder holsters and beautiful false-eyelashed women carrying coffee carafes.

Napolean and Illya didn't bother to wait to arrive at headquarters to drink coffee. A favorite coffee moment occurs right at the start of The Odd Man Affair. David McCallum, as Illya darts out of his New York jazz lp-filled apartment brandishing a coffee cup and, still sipping, slips neatly into Robert Vaughn's (Solo's) convertible. It is obvious that they are late. Moments later they drive up inside the UNCLE garage, where they do gun battle with some enemy THRUSH agents. Although the coffee cup disappears in order for Illya to shoot two or three of the jack-booted thugs, his coffee-charged bravado carries him proudly when, surveying the mass of bodies he and his comrade have just eliminated, he deadpans, "We haven't even signed in yet."

My parents always tried to stop my watching Dobie Gillis. I don't know why this particular program ranked so low in their book. I remember my mother voicing concerns that young people might "get the wrong" idea watching Maynard G. Krebs, Bob Denver's beatnik character. Naturally, we watched every episode, although the only striking memory I have is of seeing cans of coffee in father Herbert T. Gillis' corner grocery stacked behind a sign advertising $.99 per pound prices. I always longed for a scene where Maynard would introduce us to his beatnik friends at a coffee shack, but somehow the show's producers failed to utilize Maynard as anything but a way-out loner, with no other links to the subculture but his dress and scruff-beard.

At the other end of the unreality spectrum, there was Hazel. Hazel was an already out-of-date character developed in the post World War II G.I. promise/fantasy of upper-middle class luxury for having beaten both Germany and Japan. My parents both watched this program, laughing buckets when Shirley Booth ran her buxom frame at trot-speed in response to any irrational requests from her scatterbrained family employers. My wheelchair-ridden grandmother skipped her nightly medication to remain awake for this program, adding her own narration, reproaching the program from afar as it presented this or that detail of servant behavior as a kind of unpaid technical consultant and as a painful reminder to my mother of the days past when our family supposedly held a staff of domestic help, rather than the kitchen full of electric appliance "help" my mother had to depend on. Hazel's shoddy coffee making methods offered further evidence in the decline of household staff quality. Booth, attempting to add sweeping wide-eyed Lucy-like voice and mannerisms to "spike" every line, appeared not to pay any attention to how many scoops of canned coffee she spooned into the by-then standard electric percolator. Here's hoping the coffee was better served at the inevitable family therapy sessions where this dysfunctional broadcast clan must have gone, maid and all.

Coffee was best left to the working class, after all, television's real audience backbone. While Hazel's boss hardly touched his coffee, Dragnet's Joe Friday took his coffee like communion, especially in the series' 1950s heyday. First with partner Ben Romero (shot and killed in the series after actor Barton Yarborough died of a heart attack) and then with Frank Smith, Friday lived on coffee and cigarettes, a diet no longer fashionable. Unlike modern police methods, Friday always produced the right suspect, with airtight evidence and likely a fully signed confession, although the use of a high intensity lamp aimed directly at the suspect's beady eyes seemed to help.

Jack Webb's staccato production style seldom allowed for close-up shots of coffee making, but when he and a sidekick poured themselves a steaming cup in their squad car during a stake out, you knew it was good and strong. No matter how many cups, Friday never had the coffee jitters. If he did, he knew he could release them by taking an extra long puff on a filterless Camel cigarette, or by delivering one of his famous clipped line of sarcasm to a reluctant witness, always to the nods of everyone present. I like to picture Webb, night creature, sitting in a late night coffee bar, sipping hot java (even his first name was Joe, slang for coffee) in his trench coat. My dream, by the way, is still in vivid black and white. Later Webb shows, filmed in weak color, fail to provide any of the atmosphere of the early series. It may be my imagination, but I don't think there's much coffee, either.

A lot of people have found memories of *Bonanza*, but not me. I remember it being on Sunday night, which was right before Monday's school week began. Wrestling with bouts of depression looking towards another week of imprisonment, I felt little affection for this all-male ranching family. Their coffee came

Great Coffee

from stovetop pots, indicating the were boiling the brew. There is no romance in any aspect of old West coffee making.

I couldn't really pretend to discuss television's treatment of coffee without mentioning that 60s angel of bad coffee making and domestic meddler, Folgers' Mrs. Olson, played by some bad actress whose name escapes me. The script was the same for all these ads: A 60s housewife, distraught at having her lack of social and culinary skills exposed before her husband's boss/mother/golf buddy is about to fall apart behind the kitchen door, when in comes this smiling patron saint of middle brow entertaining, Mrs. Olson. The young woman moans that she's never made good coffee (the most believable piece of dialogue contained) and now is compelled to perform. Does Mrs. Olson glare over at the electric percolator and accompanying can of supermarket swill and growl, "There's your problem!"? Of course not. In true corporate form, Mrs. Olson, trademarked "Svedish" accent in high gear, assures her tenderly that there's no secret to making good coffee. Then she ushers her young charge back into the living room and proceeds, I believe, to pull a small sack of beans out of her purse and probably hand grind them and brew them using a vacuum coffee maker. All the audience knows is a few frames later, in walks Mrs. Olson with a percolator (no doubt as a serving vessel) full of fresh made coffee. Hubby, realizing it's the weekend and he's bubbling with testosterone, looks over at his wife and exclaims "Honey, that's the best coffee I've ever had..

Not fully content to remain a back room consultant, Mrs. Olson cattily pokes a small hole in the hostess' ego, by crediting THE PRODUCT. "Folgers is mountain grown."

"Mountain grown?", cries the chorus.

"It's the richest kind," resounds Mrs. Olson, apparently satisfied that she's thwarted any kind of false glamour that might be ascribed either the hostess or the coffee maker.

It's this kind of thinking and false advertising that will someday become known as leading to the downfall of our post-World War II empire.

In recent years television seems to have been content to limit itself to products more in keeping with their audience's true sophistication, such as instant coffee.

Perhaps it's best, as I have yet to see a truly fine product or proper coffee making appear on television. Apparently, like the Irish language and freedom in

Eastern Europe, fine coffee remains a person-to-person art form best left off the tube.

COFFEE IN THE MOVIES

As someone who misspent some of his early life viewing movies and watching TV, I can't help but recall some of coffee's more memorable moments before the camera. Long before Folgers foisted the know-it-all Mrs. Olson on viewers, coffee had ingrained itself.

Here are but a few moments memorable to me:

The 1952 film noir classic, *The Turning Point* with Edmond O'Brien as a well-intentioned but naive politician trying to clean the rats out of government featured a scene with him making coffee using a vacuum maker. The film's director wisely starts the scene during the vacuum drawing the finished coffee back down into the lower carafe. I can't watch the scene without shoveling some fresh grounds into my own vacuum Silex.

For the best "coffee as a sacrament" you can't do better than *Air Mail*, my favorite John Ford film. Cheerless airline executive (wearing a flight suit) Ralph Bellamy must pour twenty cups of coffee to maintain his seemingly eternal vigil running his airmail operation during an equally endless fog-bound night. As atmospheric as these exciting early years of airborne heroics were, I think in balance I prefer the boredom of modern airlines. The safety, but not the coffee has improved, however.

Another noir classic, *The Stranger on the Third Floor*, sets much of its dark story line around the confines of a diner called Nick's. Nick, a Greek restaurateur steals a scene in which he explains the reason his coffee is so good to two dewy-eyed starlets who ask his secret. "The secret", Nick explains, "is I put a raisin in every cup." I'm thinking of remaking the film with this scene in it. It turns out that I am Nick's killer, after I discover he's been flavoring my coffee without my knowledge.

Any film with alcoholics in it is guaranteed to feature early morning "black coffee" scenes and *"Lost Weekend"* is no exception. Ray Milland's portrait of a boozer is liberally peppered with the coffee-making activities of crusading Jane Wyman, whose employment of a percolator almost excuses Milland's habit, at least in my book.

Preston Sturges, whose work seems to age even better than the best Sumatra green beans, obviously knew how to weave the coffee into a good yarn. His classic, *Christmas in July*, is about an advertising wannabe, Dick Powell, who tries to get the attention of gal pal Ellen Drew with his slogan, "If you can't sleep at night, it's not the coffee. It's the bunk." In fact, he enters the slogan in a contest sponsored by a major coffee company. At one point his mother notices that he has accidentally dropped a penny in his coffee cup. "That's lucky", she says with her first generation brogue. Sorry, Mom. Not in my house, where you couldn't see a penny in the bottom of the cup, if you were to drop one in. I'd remake the coffee.

One *Coffee Companion* staffer forced me to endure the ultra-campy *Pillow Talk*. Other than watching Rock Hudson method-act love interest in Doris Day, this film does have our top-rated Chemex coffee maker as its scene stealer. Once I spotted the Chemex, I rewound and ran the scene several times.

The 70s and 80s proved to be dark ages for coffee makers, as for coffee in general. It speaks volumes about the our culture's subconscious shame in using electric percolators and switching to high-content robusta-grade coffees that there is a drought of good coffee making scenes in films during this period.

In the 90s, we had *Cafe Romeo* (a film so dependent on Joseph Campanella that even after he dies he is brought back via flashback for the film's duration). Although *Ground Hog Day* has no noteworthy coffee scenes in it, I was impressed by rumors that Bill Murray insisted on specialty coffee from a local roaster during shooting. A Christopher Walken film, *In the Company of Strangers*, has him sipping espresso in Venice while playing intense psychotic games with two impressionable Americans.

I haven't yet seen the ultimate coffee cinema scene. When I do, I'll let you know.

COFFEE BEHIND BARS

After spending years in search of the perfect cup of coffee, I must admit I've had quite a few that have come close enough to deserving to be, as the saying goes, "almost too good to be legal." And upon that flimsy premise I became curious to try the coffee given society's true illegals... the men and women who populate our expanding prison system. How good or bad is it? It would seem that it should, along with hard beds, out-of-date newspapers and small-screen television, be a part of their punishment for disobeying the law in this, the greatest country on earth.

I've certainly had coffee that seems more of a punishment than a joy here, on the outside that is. The more I thought about this the more obsessed I became, until I began introducing myself to a few lawyers and judges at parties (I normally would be embarrassed to be seen with these types) with the hidden motive of obtaining passage into the coffee klatches within the prison system.

Finally, Sid Heller, my attorney of many years, called me late one night.

Sid: Kevin, I've done it.

KS: You've been dis-barred?

Sid: I could be if this ever gets out. I've got you a visitors' pass to three institutions, a city lockup, a county jail and a Federal penitentiary. What's my Christmas present?

That's Sid. Effective and right to the point.

So, here I am writing this report on the way back from my tour of *coffee el frisko*.

CITY JAIL

My first sip of city jail's coffee said it all. In fact, it reminded me of a Beatle's Song, "Yesterday." The worst thing about it to me was that... the guards appear to be drinking it too. Now, I can almost understand some fellow who finds himself here awaiting trial having a few cups just to get through the boring courtroom tactics. After all, his lawyer has to stall the case along until everyone connected with it either dies, or can't remember. But the guards??? Frankly, I expected better. By the way, I don't suppose you can guess whose coffee they serve here. I'll give you a clue. They're getting married in their new series of television commercials. I can't believe I actually miss Mrs. Olson.

If I were ever here, I mean really here, I know I would use my one phone call to reach Charlie Sarrin at Detroit's Coffee Express. "Hello, Charlie. Kevin Sinnott here. Hey, do you suppose you could overnight some Sumatra and maybe a Chemex? I'll have to send you a check."

Oh yes, and there are insects here. Large ones.

COUNTY JAIL

I always promised my larger-than-life uncle, one Father John Dufficy, that I would never stoop so low as to use sensationalist drivel so prevalent in the newspapers. Nevertheless, I couldn't help but think of O.J. Simpson while I sat in cell block 19B at the McHenry County Court lockup. (Footnote: Some lawyer, Sid. He couldn't even swing it so I could get into the larger and more urbane Cook County Jail, which has housed some of society's most infamous scoundrels. McHenry County is mostly made up of out-of-work house painters who got into arguments with their landlords.)

It was obvious that the experience was destined to be unpleasant. The foul smelling man in the next cell noticed my customary sport coat (I did wear a striped shirt) and insisted on calling me, "English" for the duration of my stay. The guard posted for my ward asked me if he could get me anything such as cigarettes. I responded that I would like a cup of coffee, fresh if that was possible.

He gave me a queer look after that last comment, about the freshness. I was quietly glad that he did. It meant that he hadn't guessed my true identity. When my "host" returned he handed me the usual institutional styrofoam cup. Wedged alongside it was a packet of Sweet N Low, a guarantee of poor ingredients. How is it McDonalds is able to afford Equal and a big customer like the prison system can't?

I know you're getting curious about the cup quality.

Surprise. The coffee was... quite good. Aromatic. With a nice acid and medium body. The finish was the only place where the telltale signs of a less than stellar product was being used here.

Oh, I could definitely quibble about the formula. I have no doubt that they were employing the usual "one teaspoon per cup of coffee" for every cup. If I were to stay here for even one day, I would offer my recommendations that they "up" the grounds-to-water ratio.

Perhaps it was the nearby stench of my fellow inmates, but even the styrofoam cup seemed inoffensive. When I was released I noticed the coffee making station was equipped with last month's top rated Bunn coffee maker and Yuban coffee. Someone around here must have tastebuds.

STATE PEN

State penitentiaries are both the best and worst of our penal system. There are the ultra-violent "Natural Born Killer"- types who probably can't be trusted with any glass equipment for fear they will convert a broken carafe into a dangerous weapon. Then there are the so-called "county club" prisons filled with reckless stock brokers and tax evading Mafiosi, where I would half-expect commercial quality cappuccino makers, maybe even a Starbucks or Gloria Jean's franchise operating within the prison walls to serve these high-flyers.

The Illinois prison of Stateville boasts no such luxury. Even though I was allowed into only the minimum security areas, much of the coffee appeared to be instant. The guards here definitely keep to themselves. They do not share coffee or any other informalities with the prisoners. My rather limited contact with the other prisoners didn't allow me to become "wise" to any sort of underground "specialty coffee" system such as exists for cigarettes, and "you-name-it"... I did notice one Gavalia package on the window sill of an inmate. But for all I know, it was a birthday present from his aunt. I was unable to find its owner, who was probably in the gymnasium during my stay.

In case anyone's interested, I discovered that prison terms - I guess I should say, prison phrases, such as calling the guards "screws", guns "rods" or "heaters" and the other inmates "bud" or "pal" are apparently no longer in style. The first time I attempted to use any of these in passing conversation, a hearty round of laughter resulted. I apologized and covered my ignorance by claiming I had been transferred from an older prison community. The prisoners took it in stride, and told me I'd seen too many Humphrey Bogart films.

Great Coffee

TASTER'S CHOICE: NOT MUCH

There are basically three choices of state penn brews. First, there is the institutional coffee served at breakfast and dinner. Frankly, it tasted identical to what I'd been served on AMTRAK. It had Nestles written all over it. The harsh assault on the tongue, the weak body and the sour aftertaste. I'm sure by the urns they were using (verified by "Mel", who works kitchen duty or mess, as he calls it). The second choice is to drink coffee from a vending machine. Here the coffee is probably technically worse than the stuff in the hall, but for some reason, it actually offered more in overall perception. I was unable to bring in any laboratory equipment to verify brew strength, but I would say their machine was extracting better than average. The coffee actually had some of the finer notes of a decent high-grown arabica, rather than the robusta in the "mess".

The third method is to have coffee with "Charlie". Charlie is an inmate who actually has his own coffee maker. Charlie also uses decent coffee, by prison standards. Charlie uses Yuban, too. (What's this thing about Yuban and prisons?) And he brews it strong, at least fairly strong. Charlie is also allowed to get bottled water, because the guards didn't want him to carry the glass carafe back and forth to the water fountain. Charlie says it makes better coffee, which, I basically agree with.

I think Charlie used to work in a supermarket. I'm not sure whether he said he had a job in a supermarket or he pulled a job in one.

Charlie makes a pretty fair cup, though, under the circumstances. He also told me he hates kids and is a member of Greenpeace.

CONCLUSIONS

First, I would advise no one to go to prison to taste the coffee or otherwise. I certainly don't miss being there, even if it was just for "the experiment." If I ever get in trouble I will pay Sid whatever he asks to try to stay out.

But... the coffee in prison, overall, is no worse, and even in some important ways, better generally, than that in most outside venues.

The coffee may be cheap in the mess, but, due to time limitations on meal service, the coffee never "stayed up past its bedtime" on scalding hot plates or suffered a slow death in an airpot.

Rainy Day Features

The county coffee was actually near exceptional for food service. It would put most office coffee service to shame.

Many air travelers suffer far more for being coffee drinkers than men and women who have broken the law and are supposed to be punished for it.

There oughta be a law.

MY CHRISTMAS CUP

"Watch out for that boy. He's too nice. I can see he's up to no good."

My mother always warned me about Sid Heller. He's kind of like a live one-man roadshow version of Eddie Haskell. So why do I still fall for his dares without question? I guess it's the nature of friendship. We are all victims and punishers. And, I must say this for Sid, my lawyer: He always manages to get me out of the many jams his advice and counsel lands me in.

Take last Christmas. Sid and I were at a cocktail party his firm give to all their favorite clients. I guess I must rate, although I am really small potatoes compared to some of their corporate accounts. I'm sure I'm only invited because I'm at least an adept conversationalist, a trait Sid's on-staff fellow patent attorneys seem to lack.

Anyway, there were Sid and I.

I was in the middle of arguing with Sid about the basic goodness of humans, as good a Christmas party argument as any. Sid suddenly came up with an interesting idea.

"Kev, why don't you test your own theory about the basic charity of people yourself, the way you test coffee makers?"

"What?" I stammered, trying to remember Mother's advice about never listening to Sid's ideas.

Sid insisted, "Here's what I'm saying: Just go stand outside a cafe and ask patrons for enough money for a cup of coffee."

"What will that prove?" I was getting a little hot, especially the way Sid managed to combine his idea with my favorite beverage that way.

"It will prove that coffee drinkers, just like the rest of us, are selfish and uncaring. If you are forced to drink only at the charity of your fellow man, or woman, you will go thirsty, my friend."

This was too much. A female onlooker at the party accepted the challenge on my - er, behalf. I was to feign that I needed money for coffee. No, I wouldn't mock the homeless. I would dress in my usual way. I chose some worn pants, a pullover sweatshirt and scuffed shoes. I also decided to remain fashionably unshaven, just like George Michael. I basically wore the "I was an engineer at AT&T until a few years ago when I was laid off" look, which has really caught on. Unfortunately, I don't think I stood out quite enough, although I did make about thirty dollars in one morning. There was one brief almost-embarrassing moment when I noticed a chum from my club ambling my way. As he drew near, I reneged on my pledge not to imitate the homeless and shouted, *Streetwise*, the name of a local paper sold by the homeless. That was all it took to make my acquaintance look away as he passed. I took a deep breath and a dollar from a young woman who then expected me to produce her copy of *Streetwise*. When I didn't have one, she snapped her dollar back in disgust, realizing I was a fakir.

Next day, I was back, only this time I chose both a better form of dress and a better neighborhood. I positioned myself at the inside entrance of a small cafe located inside a Loop (the real downtown, not Lincoln Park) office building basement. There are a number of these indoor malls in Chicago's vast network of underground links between office buildings. At first I was unlucky in that the attractive "barista" kept insisting on keeping me in Lattés (this spend-thrifty bleeding heart wanted me to have the most expensive drink). I finally broke down and told her my mission. Afterwards she ignored me beautifully, so that I might hustle a little, while inside the warmth of her store. Keep in mind that I have no experience doing this. The last time I did anything remotely like it was as a Salvation Army volunteer several years ago. And, by comparison that is a completely passive activity. No lying. Just the bell.

However, I did all right for an amateur. In fact, I would say that the average customer was quite generous. Except most of my business was not exactly cash. Many invited me to join them in their repast. I sipped (or began to sip) nearly twenty cups of coffee that day. I felt like a tester at Folgers, only with better coffees to test. Around 3 P.M. after another round with three female workers from a twelfth floor accounting firm, the barista, Wendy, leaned over and whispered, "You'd better take it easy. You're getting pretty wound up". Suddenly, Chelsea, one of my new found acquaintances, burst out, "Hey, you've left your wallet at home. How're you going to get home tonight?" Whereupon a collection was taken and I got not only train fare, but they made sure I had enough for the afternoon paper.

Christmas day was approaching and I realized my experiment must soon end. It was part of the bet. Besides Sid would be over Christmas day. He spends every Christmas at my house. Sid's Jewish, but he says he comes over just to see "how the goyum spend Christmas." He can't fool me. He likes the sense of togetherness, at least when we don't argue. My brother John always argues. Not just at Christmas either. Of course, Sid likes to argue with the best of them.

My last effort was made at a shopping mall. I was there on a Saturday morning, just one week before the holiday. Shoppers were dropping in for a mid-morning fortification. The enclosed mall allowed me the option of standing in complete comfort near but not in a coffee shop. I had learned to go for cash rather than risk another day overindulging.

Things were going quite well. Then, who should walk up but my friend, Mike Huetson. Mike and I used to perform comedy together, going back to high school. Although I was dressed like your average privileged mortgaged-to-the-hilt shopper, Mike intuitively guessed my game. Unfortunately, he didn't guess my reason. He immediately shook my hand, looked gravely at me and inquired, "I knew you should never have gone into publishing. It ruined my grandfather you know. (Mike's grandfather published a magazine on how to invest in the stock market, turning out his first issue in-1929!)

Timing is everything.

I tried to shoo Mike away without having to go into detail. Not only was he scaring away potential "clients". I had learned quickly that every person passing by is potential and I didn't want to waste time or opportunity.

For some reason Mike was in a talkative mood that day. He was probably avoiding shopping. Suddenly my concerns became even greater as I noticed a private mall patrolman walking our way.

Mike, realizing that I was paying absolutely no attention to what he was saying, excused himself.

Great Coffee

The patrolman walked up and asked me if I was okay.

"I noticed a lady giving you some money," he explained. I responded that I'd left my wallet at home and merely got thirsty and wished to get a cup of coffee.

"Must be kind of tough shopping without a wallet," he said, fumbling with his cellular phone while we spoke.

I felt uneasy. I hadn't thought of that. He was right of course. Why would I stay in a mall, if I didn't have my wallet? I decided to try the old number 7.

"My wife walked off with it," I explained, trying to maintain good eye contact, knowing how important it is when you're lying. "I'm supposed to meet her for lunch and she's late as usual. Probably busy charging."

"That's good for business," he confided. "The spenders built this place. Did you get your coffee money?" he asked.

"Enough for a small".

"It's Christmas," he smiled. Then producing a few one dollar bills, he said, "Get yourself a Grande."

I realized Sid was wrong. The giving spirit lives.

Merry Christmas.

Coffee Gallery

Chapter Fifteen

Coffee on the Web

Pan-American Coffee
Bureau circa 1953

Coffee is there... While they're reaching for a star

Coffee Inspiration

"But the greatest among you shall be your servant." Matthew 23:11

To me, one of the great reasons for coffee's success in the world is it is a great way to serve someone. I truly enjoy taking the time to make and share coffee with a visitor. I get a chance to fuss over this person, whomever they are. It's one of the few cooking arts where men and women are equals. Fortunately, the rituals are simple enough to allow me to remain a participant. Which of us doesn't feel a little better when someone goes out of their way for us?

15

Coffee on the Web

Coffee and the web go together like cream and sugar. It makes perfect sense.

As much as I admire the wine connoisseur, it is difficult to imagine someone throwing back several glasses from their collection and surfing the web. It's neither the image nor the physical reality of the hobby.

Coffee, however, enables the high-speed modem in each of us. I enjoy coffee with friends, but I also find that myself brewing a one-cup and going online is its own ritual.

Naturally, the coffee lover is interested in every subject. But, there are some very enjoyable web sites that are particularly suited to coffee itself.

Here is a list directly copied from my favorites web list:

Flying Saucers Coffee – fun coffee site. My own interest in UFO's gives me a warm feeling, even though I've never tasted the product. I would expect it to be out of this world.

Old Coffee Roasters (oldcoffeeroasters.com/robots.htm) – A great site for lovers of the vacuum coffee makers (like me!) Old ads, instruction manuals, I'd rate this one the best.

Coffee Biz (coffeebiz.com) – the Roastery Development Group is a romantic's business group. They are a virtual coffee business flea market – I mean that as a compliment.

Coffeeteaabout.com – where else on the web can you see a downloadable video of an espresso shot being poured in order to improve your technique. One shot (pun intended) show, but worth a visit. It really is useful.

Lucidcafe – a web mall, including a for-profit web site featuring bean reviews by my friend and colleague Ken Davids. As much as I like Ken, I'd say buyer beware, this site is designed to sell merchandise. I'd say the same thing even if I developed a web site that reviewed…and sold beans. There are also some problems with coffee bean reviews, since so much of a coffee's flavor is influenced by the brewing method. Still, worth a visit.

Hariousa.com – a great product that virtually died on the vine in the before the web, the Hario vacuum maker is a fine one. The web is perfect for an obscure product like this.

Too Much Coffee Man – an insider's comic strip but a fun one if coffee is a big part of your life.

Coffeecompanion.com – my site if you want to browse around.

Coffee Gallery

Chapter Sixteen

Great Coffee Questions and Answers

Pan-American Coffee
Bureau circa 1953

Give yourself a coffee break

Letters to Kevin Sinnott

Dear Mr. Sinnott,
Is coffee known as an aphrodisiac?
Candy, Millers Grove MT

Dear Candy,
Is coffee an aphrodisiac... or is it that more passionate and sensitive people are attracted to coffee? I pondered your question all last evening in my library. I can find no reliable data on the subject. However, there are volumes of anecdotal literature proclaiming coffee as a precursor to romance.

Dear Kevin,

Thanks for the French press review, conducted with your usual irreverence and technical accuracy. Someone should develop a French press in a thermal container. Meanwhile, fellow fanatics might find my technique useful - I simply heat a pot of water on the stove at the same time I start a kettle. When the kettle boils, I turn off both burners, scald the press, load it and fill it, then set it in the open pot of hot water. This maintains a very even brew temperature throughout the extraction (never below 190F) and gives great results. I felt you came down pretty hard on the French press in your review. I use mine all the time and I've always found it brewed a great cup of coffee, sediment and all. What's wrong with liking a coffee maker that also looks cool?
Bert, Salt Lake City, UT

Dear Bert,
I'll work backwards. There's nothing wrong with like a cool-looking coffee maker. Unfortunately, I don't think it's my job to

be some kind of art critic for industrial design. I also like the press' design, for what it's worth. As far as liking the maker, I thought I was pretty kind. My mother raised me to be honest, as well. The press' temperatures do fall below supposedly proper standards unless you prescald it before brewing and heat it during brewing. The sediment may not bother you but it does some people. I thought they had a right to know.

Dear Kevin:

I loved your article about coffee on television. You're a great writer. As a Star Trekkie, I couldn't let my favorite coffee moment pass without telling you. In the episode, The Trouble With Tribbles, Dr. McCoy finds a tribble in his coffee cup.

Keep up the good work. Don't ever worry about being called a nerd. I like that in a man. It reminds me of Mr. Spock.

Dana, Minneapolis, MN

Dear Dana,

Who called me a nerd? Has my high school coach been gossiping at the nursing home? Thanks for the Trek memory. I figured I'd let the Trekkies fill me in. I've seen that episode but didn't remember it.

Dear Kevin,

I was surprised that you said in your grinder review that ideally all coffee grounds should be equal in size. I believe there is a reason that is not the goal, in that equal sized particles would re-bond and stop up the drip process. I know that at Dallis Brothers, we actually add back a certain amount of fines (small particles) to meet the spec (specification). Perhaps you or Doctor Illy could explain?

David Dallis, Dallis Coffee, NY

Questions and Answers

Dear David,

Thanks for the letter. Before we get started, I cannot afford a doctor, having used up my insurance benefits this year. First, I did say that, as far as flavor is concerned, the best ground coffee would consist of completely even-size particles. This is because the window for ideal extraction is narrow and neither under or over-extracted grounds serve us. The under-extracted grounds are a product waste and the overextracted grounds cause bitterness. When most people try to brew proper full-strength coffee at home after grinding with a poor grinder, they suffer from having over-extracted fine grounds in the mess. The fines also slow extraction, doubling the difficulty.

I know of no evidence that evenly ground coffee would cause a perfect fitting grounds bed that would become stopped up. As long as the shapes are irregular, it would seem desirable for flow.

As far as the industry specification, I expect adding fines back into the coffee is designed to reduce product waste. It may also be a standardization, a term often used to bring the overall quality lower in order to be equal to lesser products. As for my coffee, David, you can skip adding the fines back in. I challenge anyone, especially in our scientific readership to add to our discussion.

Kevin

Dear Kevin,

I found your *Coffee Companion* newsletter at our public library. This is a great read. How come Starbucks doesn't stock it? Have you ever tried the Bosch Home espresso maker? If yes, then how did it rank?

Marcy, Cambridge Mass

Dear Marcy,

Believe it or not, Starbucks was very close to carrying us throughout the chain. At the eleventh hour, they held a several hour meeting, where one or two executives decided it might be unwise, because we "would not necessarily review only items found at their stores." I could have guaranteed that I would never favor them or anyone. I have found it is a rare retailer who has the long-term interest in coffee and the ego management that allows them to place unfiltered information such as we present in their stores.

Item #2, the Bosch machine. Yes, I tried it. The idea was unique and clever, that of a centrifugal force to develop extraction pressure for espresso. Unfortunately, the idea was either unsound, or their practical engineering was off. The thing never made cups that bore more than a passing resemblance to the real cafe item, a great shame.

Dear Kevin,

I saw you on 20/20 as part of a story on caffeine addiction. I believe I am addicted to coffee. Do you run a self-help group? If so, I might join. What are the dues?

Gwen, Philadelphia, PA

Dear Gwen,

Turning to me to help you stop drinking coffee is like hanging around with Joe Camel to stop smoking. However, I am not addicted to all coffee, just the best. If you are really seriously concerned about your health, contact a local health professional, who is waiting to take your money. Good luck.

Dear Kevin,

I read about two scientists in Texas who developed a coffee strength control. What happened? Did it work?

Sam, Seattle, WA

Sam, what a pleasure to get a letter from your town that doesn't recount the origins of retail-Mall espresso. That coffee strength control was designed to monitor the brew strength in the carafe and signal the maker to stop brewing once the coffee reached a certain "weakness" (remember, drip coffee is stronger initially and gets weaker with more water). One problem, of course, is that this means a consumer can no longer be guaranteed to get eight cups, as the volume will vary. The unit read light, which is a good idea. As far as I know, no company has yet

Questions and Answers

introduced a maker (it was tested on a Braun coffee maker in development). I'd like to see it utilized and I have my own ideas as to its best application.

Dear Kevin,

I saw you speak at Coffee Fest in Minneapolis. Very funny and interesting. I am new to coffee and am opening my own cafe. I was amazed when I saw you later that evening in a restaurant, walking out of the kitchen wearing an apron, apparently demonstrating the right way to serve coffee to the manager and his staff. You are obviously committed. But, aren't you afraid you'll be committed?

Angel, Minneapolis

Dear Angel,

I am absolutely committed to the creation and enjoyment of well-brewed coffee. What you observed was simply some play-acting as a demonstration to that restaurateur of some valuable tips on brewing and then promptly serving the coffee. Too bad you weren't in the kitchen a moment before, where I was wearing a chef's hat and making the beverage. I may seem a little unconventional by the standards of the corporate let's-play-it-safe school. But convincing an entire industry to upgrade its methods demands strong and unconventional tactics. Nobody was hurt and that restaurant may be serving better coffee. I know they'll never forget me.

Dear Kevin,

I couldn't believe it when you told me about *Fresh Cup* and *Coffee Talk* in your e-mail reply regarding my new cafe. I thought publishers were all in competition. Thanks for you enlightened attitude. My only question is: how do you stay in business?

Eileen, Ottawa, Canada

Dear Madam,

That is how I stay in business. I sell information, not exclusivity. You know, there used to be a country called The Soviet Union that went out of business trying to limit what people read. Just for the record, there are a number of trade and consumer coffee publications. I have my favorites regarding this or that purpose, but they all serve a segment, usually one better than anyone else. There's *Cups* up in Canada, as well as the glossy *Coffee Journal* here in the U.S. There's *World Coffee and Tea, Specialty Coffee Retailer* and *Gourmet Retailer* (less coffee than foods but they cover both.) Oh, and don't forget *The Coffee And Tea Trade Journal*, the oldest one in the U.S. and where I also have the privilege of being a columnist on trade issues.

Dear Kevin,

Where does that word Jamoch come from? I've heard it in 1930s films and I know it has a coffee meaning, but it's lost on me. I saw you on the Food Channel. You seem like someone who might know its true meaning.

Wendy R, Seattle, WA

Dear Wendy,

As always in the game of word detective, there's probably a certain amount of nonsense. For instance, "hard as nails." Nails are certainly hard, but the real meaning appears to come from a Civil War General, General Nails, who was a particularly demanding leader. Now, onto your question: I believe the word jamoch comes from the combination of java and mocha. You may be interested to know that during the first half of the century consumers were very loyal to this blend. The one thing I can't answer is exactly why someone began referring to another as a jamoch, but I also have heard actors such as W.C. Fields and others use the term.

Dear Mr Coffee,

Why is coffee always stale in the can? Is it because the shelf life is shorter? Or do they just let the cans sit in a warehouse forever before they ship it?

Walter B, Philadelphia, PA

Questions and Answers

Dear Sir,

Coffee must be packed stale or the can will buckle from the release of carbon dioxide. In fact, the process is called staling. Years ago, when the cans were made of heavier steel (many are now made of other metals) the staling process was less. Consequently, the canned coffees were fresher when you got them. Consumers could pressure the large companies to improve the cans but the matter is becoming a moot point. The trend is now to pack the preground coffee in one-way valve bags that allow the coffee to be packed as soon as it is cool enough to leave the roaster. The valve allows any carbon dioxide gas to leave whenever it desires.

Dear Editor,

I read with interest your Braun Flavor Select review. I must say I was disappointed. You seemed to feel it was neither fish nor fowl. Why?

Mehta, Fish Creek, WI

Dear Mehta,

The reason I was in the middle on this issue is simply one of honesty. I am in the middle. I really feel that the Braun is a good attempt to do something different. But, no, it is not wholly able to satisfy my demanding palate.

Dear Kevin,

Why don't you rate coffees? I really respect your opinion, and you are very good at reviewing the hardware. You should really tell us where the best coffees are.

Geena, Hollywood, CA

Dear Geena,

Rating coffees is like rating works of art to me. I just don't see the point. The equipment to resolve coffee flavors is designed to meet objectives. I feel it is more relevant to point out whether it can do so. Meanwhile, I would like to take this opportunity to give my friend Kenneth Davids a plug. He has been hired to rate coffees for a new newsletter, *Coffee Review*. Not the most original title, but it is literally what you have asked for.

Dear Mr Coffee,

I have searched all over for the Flavor Seal Vacuum coffee maker. It seems that the specialty stores in my area just carry the standard Krups machines or, at best, the French press. Any suggestions?

Pete Portland, OR

Dear Pete:

Whenever I review equipment, I provide a phone number for the manufacturer. Until I decide to sell equipment (hopefully never) you will have to call the manufacturer directly. The subsurface part of your question is, of course, why don't some specialty retailers take more of an interest in the coffee hardware (forgive the computer analog)? First, many coffee retailers are first and foremost roasters who are concerned more with the quality of their roasting equipment, and perhaps commercial brewing if they provide in-store drinks. The other challenge specific to coffee is the lack of profit margin in coffee equipment. Unlike almost any other industry, the money is coffee is in the drinks first, and the beans second. Coffee making equipment is a distant third. Hence equipment is grudgingly carried. The otherwise obscure French press is widely available due to its low manufacture cost and its substantial markup. The Flavor Seal is a high cost and high price unit, virtually the kiss of death in terms of retail acceptance, although, as you point out, it is a superb performer.

Dear Kevin,

My boyfriend and I both love coffee. Which sex makes better coffee? I respect your opinion on this. What do you think?

Margie, Austin, TX

Questions and Answers

Dear Margie,

First, I detest the current need to pit men and women in a chronic contest. To use some new age terms, I am more feminine in my desire to see coffee making as a cooperative art rather than a competitive battle. One of the most refreshing observations I've made about coffee is it is truly a multi-cultural experience. I happen to make the coffee in most of my relationships, due to my intense history as a connoisseur, and lately, because of my new found media prominence. My advice to couples is to put the task above the need for sexual identification. Coffee making, like making love or prayer, is best an act of mutual enjoyment and effort. This is as close to spiritual or adult-oriented prose as I hope I ever get.

Dear Kevin,

I loved your "Coffee in the Movies" article. Have you ever seen *Harper*? In the first scene, Paul Newman wakes up in his detective office and makes coffee in a Chemex using yesterday's grounds. How about a sequel.

Oren, NY

I agree with you, Oren. By the way, your coffee beans are pretty good, too (Oren owns Oren's Daily Roast in New York - praise like that deserves a mention). I rented the Harper film upon your recommendation. I found the scene you describe to be beautifully horrifying to any coffee lover. Of course, the rest of the film is anti-climactic. Filmmaker Rule: Never begin a movie with a Chemex, save it for later in the plot.

Yes, a "Son of..." sequel is in the works.

Dear Mr Coffee,

I like here in Georgia. I happen to love coffee. How can I get the best without moving to Seattle?

Malou, Atlanta

Dear Sir,

Let's get this straight, Malou. There is not chain link fence built around any country, region, or neighborhood that contains the "best" coffee. There are good and bad cups in every town. I just spent a late night on-line, cheering up a barista in Seattle who was looking to move your way to flee from having to learn to drip foam into the shapes of movie stars faces to crest the tops of the lattés served at her store. To be accurate, you have a superb roaster just outside Atlanta, John Martinez, one whom Seattle would be lucky to have. Stop pining for a transfer. Think globally, drink locally.

Dear Kevin/Coffee Companion,

What does "natural decaf mean? What could possibly be natural about removing caffeine? Isn't all coffee naturally caffeinated?

Chris, Schaumburg, IL

Dear Chris,

All coffee is no longer caffeinated. Both Hawaii and Colombia are reported to be developing decaffeinated coffee trees. The latest player in this is Madagascar, where some naturally grown decaf is being sold and marketed. I haven't yet cupped it for flavor, but rumors are that it is poor quality. Meanwhile, natural decaf usually means that the unnatural act of decaffeinating the coffee was performed using natural ingredients. Swiss water, for instance, is a hot water bath where green unroasted coffee beans are soaked, removing all the caffeine and much of the flavor as well. General Foods uses sparkling water, a better process. It's a shame that the specialty industry really has no access to sparkling water for the very best beans. I once had a sample of sparkling water decaf that was the closest I've ever had to regular coffee. For the present, the best tasting and available process is still the unnatural methyline chloride.